Popular Mechanics

— WHEN —
DUCT TAPE
JUST ISN'T ENOUGH

Popular Mechanics

WHEN DUCT TAPE JUST ISN'T ENOUGH

QUICK FIXES FOR EVERYDAY DISASTERS

By C. J. Petersen

HEARST BOOKS
New York

HEARST BOOKS
New York

An Imprint of Sterling Publishing
387 Park Avenue South
New York, NY 10016

Popular Mechanics is a registered trademark of Hearst Communications, Inc.

Every effort has been made to ensure that all the information in this book is accurate. However, due to differing conditions, tools, and individual skills, the publisher cannot be responsible for any injuries, losses, and/or other damages that may result from the use of the information in this book.

ISBN 978-1-61837-055-6
Interior design by Agustin Chung
Cover design by Jon Chaiet
Illustrations by John Stislow, Eric Cole

Library of Congress Cataloging-in-Publication Data
Petersen, C.J.
Popular mechanics when duct tape just isn't enough Quick fixes for everyday
disasters / C.J. Petersen
    p. cm.
    Includes index.
ISBN-13: 978-1-58816-565-7
1. Home economics. 2. Dwelling—Maintenance and repair. 3. Household
appliances—Maintenance and repair. I. Popular mechanics (Chicago, III : 1959)
II. Title. III. Title: When duct tape just isn't enough.
TX145.P48 2007
643'.7—dc22

2007007693

Distributed in Canada by Sterling Publishing
c/o Canadian Manda Group, 165 Dufferin Street
Toronto, Ontario, Canada M6K 3H6
Distributed in Australia by Capricorn Link (Australia) Pty. Ltd.
P.O. Box 704, Windsor, NSW 2756, Australia

For information about custom editions, special sales, and premium and corporate purchases, please
contact Sterling Special Sales at 800-805-5489 or specialsales@sterlingpublishing.com.

Manufactured in China

2 4 6 8 10 9 7 5 3 1

www.sterlingpublishing.com

CONTENTS

There are two types of people in the world: those who know what to do when something gets busted and those who are always asking the first group for help. We offer this book as a survival manual to anyone who's in the second group—after reading it, you may just end up in the first!

There are already shelves and shelves of books that cover large home-improvement projects—replacing all the tile in a bathroom; installing new countertops in the kitchen—but there is scant information about the smaller and often more frustrating day-to-day problems that crop up around the house. You'll be hard-pressed find out how to replace just one bathroom tile that has been fractured or fix the bubble in the laminate countertop that popped up right before a dinner party.

These are the everyday dilemmas and "disasters" we face much more often than we tackle complete renovation projects. They range from the serious to the merely annoying, but all are cause for concern to those who care about their homes and yards. This book offers a real-world resource with straightforward solutions to those common problems.

Whether you're looking for a fast stopgap repair for a leaking pipe, or want a simple, inexpensive way to keep varmints from pillaging your garden, you'll find it in these pages. We've gathered the best shortcuts we could find. These are clever and easy insights from those who have tackled all the things that can go wrong around the house and come away wiser for the experience.

All quick fixes share some common factors. First, they are all fairly simple. Technical complexity and "quick fix" are mutually exclusive. Second, they are ingenious. Many of these involve using ordinary repair materials in unusual ways, or unusual materials to make conventional repairs. That makes them fun and interesting as well as useful. Lastly, these are economical ideas—most of these will save you money. A quick cleaning of the dryer vent pipe can restore dryer function and save you a hefty service-call fee. Using simple graphite lubricant can often rescue a lockset so that you don't have to foot the bill for a replacement. In reality, if you use this book to fix ten of your own everyday disasters, you'll probably have saved the cost of the book, and then some.

But just so we're clear, it's the nature of many of these solutions that they aren't permanent. A number of the fixes you'll find here are designed to help you get through an emergency until you can make a more permanent repair.

Of course sometimes that means calling a pro, or actually replacing—rather than fixing—a troublesome appliance. To help you make those key decisions, we've included several special sections that guide you to the repairman when a professional solution is the wisest option, describe how to stay safe around your own dilemmas and disasters, how to prevent disasters from occurring in the first place, and much more.

But we think perhaps the biggest benefit of *When Duct Tape Just Isn't Enough, Quick Fixes for Everyday Disasters* is that we're putting the power back in your hands. The inventive solutions presented in this book help you deal with problems as they arise, without having to run to the phone and seek overpriced help every time something goes wrong. When you're able to handle problems on your own, you feel more in control of your home and your life, which is a crucial part of the *Popular Mechanics* philosophy.

So, when dilemmas or disasters strike, pick up this book and turn to the section you need. Your own quick fix is only the flip of a page away.

—The Editors of Popular Mechanics

THE TALE OF THE TAPE:
Duct Tape, the Universal Tool

If you've tackled unexpected household repairs, you know that having a roll of that familiar gray duct tape is like an ace up your sleeve, or a safety net beneath you. Incredibly versatile, durable and strong, duct tape was developed by the Johnson & Johnson Permacel Division for the U.S. military during World War II. The army needed a tough tape to keep moisture out of ammo boxes but they, and the American public, got a virtual all-in-one solution. It quickly became popular with everyone from the guys patching up jeeps to foot soldiers who needed a quick field repair for well-worn boots.

Formed from three layers comprised of a resilient plastic skin, fiber-mesh interior, and rubber-based adhesive, the tape stays stuck even under extremely wet conditions, a property that accounts for its original nickname "Duck Tape." The name eventually morphed to duct tape during the postwar building boom when contractors used it to secure heating and cooling ductwork.

In the years since, homeowners everywhere have come to know it simply as the ideal stopgap solution to just about every crisis. There are few broken things that can't be mended with duct tape. It has secured loose appliance panels, covered windshield cracks, sealed drafty siding, patched leaking hoses, kept furniture legs in place while glue dried, and so much more. All of which makes it an essential addition to any quick-fix toolbox.

Even when the repairs you need to make are quick and simple, it pays to be prepared. For a modest investment, you can set yourself up with a basic tool kit and an emergency kit that will always be there when and if you ever need them.

The Quick and Cheap, Cheat-Disaster Tool Kit

Sure, you may already have a complete set of home-repair tools, from dozens of screwdrivers to three sizes of pipe wrench. But you can still benefit from a portable, all-in-one tool kit with just the basics you need to handle a quick fix on site. And if you are a less than well-equipped, novice do-it-yourselfer, then this type of kit is a good place to start getting yourself prepared for any kind of repair.

The idea behind a simple quick-fix tool kit is to include tools that offer multiple functions. Any one of these may not be exactly the tool you would choose for a given task, but they will be able to serve in place of a number of different tools.

+ Vise-grip pliers
+ Quick-change screwdriver with interchangeable straight and Phillips-head tips
+ Measuring tape
+ Level
+ Claw hammer
+ Assortment of screws and nails in a travel box
+ Needlenose pliers
+ Utility knife
+ $1/2$ in.-wide cold chisel
+ Wire cutters with built-in wire stripper channel
+ 8-in. adjustable wrench
+ Cordless drill and drill-bit set
+ Pencil and small notepad
+ Glue syringe
+ Safety glasses
+ Work gloves

You should also keep a few often-used supplies in your tool kit:

+ 16-oz. tub of drywall compound
+ Multigrit package of sandpaper sheets
+ Can of 3-in-1 oil
+ Small tube of super glue
+ Small container of white glue

The Emergency Preparedness Kit

Not all disasters are created equal, and while a leaking roof may present some immediate challenges, it's not on par with the aftermath of a hurricane or a region-wide power outage. The Boy Scouts are right: It pays to be prepared. Even if it never happens to you, history teaches us nothing if not the importance of planning for the worst. A simple emergency kit can provide everything you need when big disasters hit. Equip it with the following:

+ Flashlight
+ Battery-operated radio
+ Five gallons of drinking water in bottles or jugs, for each member of the household
+ Extra batteries
+ Enough canned food or packaged nonperishable food for several days
+ Candles and matches
+ Warm blankets
+ Change of clothes for each member of the household
+ A basic first-aid kit

Keep these supplies in a clean, dry area that will be easy to reach in an emergency. For a more comprehensive list of extra supplies and equipment that may be of use, check out the Department of Homeland Security's website for emergency planning at www.ready.gov.

CHAPTER 1:

TOOL TIPS

"Use the right tool for the job." That's good advice, but there are times when you just have to improvise—after all, necessity is the mother of invention, right? The pros know it's often the simplest household item that can make an existing tool work better—or substitute in a pinch for a more expensive piece of equipment you might only use once in a lifetime. You will also learn that one tool can often fulfill a completely different purpose than that for which it was originally intended. Keep an open mind to the possibilities, but remember: safety first. Don't use any tool in a reckless manner just for the sake of improvisation. Proper maintenance is probably the best tool tip of all—keep your gear safely stored and well taken care of so that every tool is working properly when you need it.

> ### DETER DETERIORATION
>
> Your tools are an investment, and you need to protect them from damaging elements, especially moisture. Keep tools in your toolbox rust free by storing a few pieces of blackboard chalk in each compartment that contains metal tools or other hardware.

1:1 GRIP EXTENSION:

You're refinishing your attic all by yourself, which means you get to wrestle with those dozen sheets of drywall.

THE QUICK FIX It's not the weight, it's the unwieldy nature of drywall sheets that makes them such a bear to move around. Carry a sheet with ease and control by tucking it under your arm and using a pry bar to grab the bottom edge.

1:2 EXTENDING YOUR REACH:

You need to slice off a bolt but your hacksaw just can't fit in the tight space.

THE QUICK FIX Grip a hacksaw blade in a pair of locking pliers to get at that hard to reach bolt or fitting that you need to saw off. The needle-nose type works even better than the standard round-jaw variety because it fits into tight spots more readily.

Bloody knuckles are your reward for rummaging through a toolbox and hitting the hacksaw blade.

THE QUICK FIX   Buy sliding binder bars (for binding reports) at a local office supply store. They are perfectly sized to slip over the blade, pinching in place to hold tight.

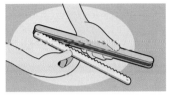

Chopping a little kindling for the fireplace is a nerve-wracking chore that severely endangers your fingers.

THE QUICK FIX   The thin pieces that are chopped up for kindling are notoriously hard to keep steady while you swing the hatchet or ax. Take a long thin scrap of wood and nail it to the top of the kindling wood, off to one side. Now you can hold the wood without ever putting your fingers near the business end of the hatchet.

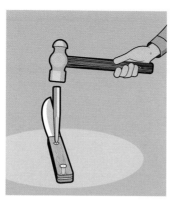

1:5 **KEEP A TIGHT GRIP:**

The riveted handle on your garden trowel has become loose, making even the simplest planting a chore.

THE QUICK FIX It's not unusual for a riveted handle to loosen, whether it's on a garden trowel, a long-handled shovel, or even a kitchen knife. Tightening the loose handle is easy. With the tool on a firm surface, strike the center of the handle rivet with a centerpunch driven by a ball-peen hammer. Don't hit it very hard, just enough to leave a small dimple. This expands the rivet slightly, taking up the slack between it and the handle.

1:6 **WEAK LINK:**

A broken or fractured link in an otherwise strong chain makes it useless for towing or securing a gate or door.

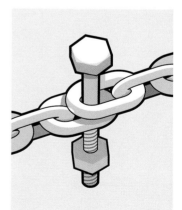

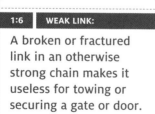

THE QUICK FIX Cut away the damaged link with a hacksaw or bolt cutters, and then join the two end links with a bolt and nut large enough for the shank to go through the center of the links without the head or nut following. This method can also be used to join two short pieces of chain to make a longer one.

You're ready to tighten a showerhead or a water line and you suddenly realize that the wrench can scar a surface as easily as it can tighten it.

THE QUICK FIX Stop a plumber's wrench from leaving its mark by wrapping chrome-plated pieces in double layers of duct tape or electrical tape before tightening them.

DISASTER PREVENTION:
Keeping a Drill from Becoming a Bad Trip

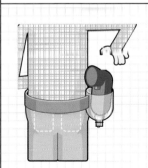

The cordless drill is a marvelous invention, but it can become an underfoot hazard when you are working on a complicated renovation project. Make a handy holster for the drill by cutting off the bottom of a plastic liter-sized soda bottle, and making two vertical cuts an inch above where the bottom was cut off. Turn the bottle upside down and thread your belt through the cut slots and you have a hip-mounted holster custom made for a cordless drill.

You're in the middle of a woodworking project and your chisel has gone dull.

THE QUICK FIX Professional woodworkers take sharpening very seriously and with good reason. Razor-sharp cutting tools work better, save time and are much safer than dull tools. But general chisel sharpening doesn't have to be quite so involved—that is, if you're willing to work with something that's not up to pro standards. Just use a piece of sandpaper—anything from 100-grit up to 220-grit will work. The coarser paper (lower number) will cut faster. The finer grit (higher number) will yield a sharper edge. Hold the paper on a hard surface and flatten the back of the chisel first. Then turn over the blade, hold the bevel side of the edge flat against the paper, and repeatedly pull the blade over the paper until the edge feels sharp. You may not be able to use the tool for shaving, but it will cut wood just fine.

THE QUICK FIX   Of the many uses to be found for sections of old garden hose, the most common involve the protection of cutting blades on all kinds of different tools like axes, hatchets, pruning saws, weeding hoes, garden scythes, and circular saws. Just cut off a piece of hose to match the length of the blade, slit it lengthwise with a utility knife, and slide the section over the blade. The hose provides plenty of protection and doesn't slip off because it tends to tightly pinch the blade. Using these protective hose coverings saves a lot of sharpening time while greatly reducing the chance of getting accidentally cut—especially important if there are children who tend to play where you store your tools.

THE QUICK FIX   You have a handy supply of readymade caps in your collection of electrical twist-on wire connectors. Just select one that fits snuggly over the dispenser tip of the glue bottle and twist it on.

Nuts, Bolts, Screws and Nails

1:11 **SCREW LOOSE:**

You're trying to replace a woodscrew, but the hole is stripped and the screw won't grab.

THE QUICK FIX Insert two short lengths of thin, insulated copper wire in the hole before adding the screw. Be sure to use stranded wire, not solid. It allows the screw to bite and is less likely to cause it to jam.

1:12 **IMMOVABLE OBJECT:**

A stubborn nut on an old lawnmower or pickup truck refuses to budge.

THE QUICK FIX The standard tactic since the dawn of the acetylene torch has been to heat the nut until it glows red. When heat alone won't cut it, touch a candle to the glowing nut. The wax will melt and flow into the threads, acting as a lubricant.

THE QUICK FIX If you don't have a screw extractor, try this trick from Douglas Adams, of Adams Construction in Brooklyn, New York, who has faced this many times. He says, "I use a lighter or match to heat the head of a nail or screw until it is red hot. [Editor's note: Grip the nail or screw with pliers to avoid burning your fingers.] Touch the head of the heated metal to the head of the painted-over screw and the paint will burn off. The heat will also make the screw expand. Cool it with a small chip of ice and it will contract, making it easier to remove."

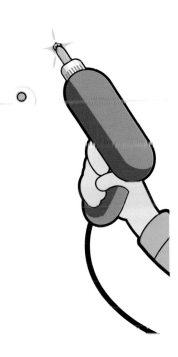

THE QUICK FIX The standard solution for "nail pops" is to drive them back into the stud. But the smart money says they'll just pop again. To ensure this doesn't happen, drive a drywall screw right above the popped nail so that the screw's head is set below the surface but doesn't puncture the paper surface. Then spackle, sand, and paint as you would with any popped nail.

1:15 **HEAD GAME:**

You're right in the middle of a small home-improvement project when the nail you're trying to pull loses its head.

THE QUICK FIX Don't lose yours. Clamp a pair of locking pliers onto the nail head then rotate the pliers so the upper or lower jaw rotates against the surface and simply bind the nail out of its hole.

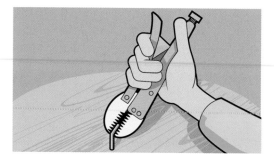

Painting Tools

1:16 **A TWO-WEEKEND PAINT JOB:**

You want to put away your paint-laden rollers and brushes without cleaning them.

THE QUICK FIX Wrap the painting utensils tightly in a plastic bag and stick them in the freezer. Once thawed, they'll be ready for use. Caveat: Paint is for painting, not eating. Be sure to seal the bag tightly to eliminate any chance of food contamination.

PAINT POLLUTION:

Even new paint can contain dirt, contaminants, or clumps that can ruin an otherwise stellar paint job.

THE QUICK FIX Make sure your paint goes on smoothly by first straining it through a square of window screen into a separate painting pail or bucket. Use rigid window screen, larger than the mouth of the bucket and dented in the middle, to sieve the paint as it drains through.

> **DISASTER PREVENTION:**
> **Catching Paint Drips**
>
> When "cutting in" while painting a ceiling, the paint eventually saturates the brush and inevitably drips down your arm—and to the floor if you're not careful. Stop the flow in its tracks by folding a small, absorbent cloth and taping it around the metal collar—known as the ferrule—of the brush. The paint will be absorbed by the cloth, which can be washed out when you're done.

> **KNOW YOUR STUFF:**
> **Paint Primers**

"Primers are the foundation to achieving a long-lasting quality paint job," says Steve Revnew, Director of Architectural Marketing, Residential Segments for Sherwin Williams. Here's a quick overview of what's what.

SURFACE	WHAT TO USE	FOR BEST RESULTS
EXTERIOR		
Unpainted exterior wood, no knots	Exterior acrylic (water-based) primer	Fill nail holes and sand before priming.
Unpainted exterior wood with defects (fungus stains, grade marks, knots)	Exterior alkyd (oil-based) stain-killing primer/sealer	Remove surface fungus with bleach /non-ammonia detergent before painting.
Unpainted exterior cedar, cypress, redwood	Exterior primer (alkyd or acrylic) rated to resist bleed-through of wood extractives	Opt for alkyd where wood shows visible bleed-through before painting.
Painted siding in good condition	Exterior acrylic primer	Siding must be clean and dry before priming.
Painted siding in poor condition with chalk	Exterior penetrating alkyd primer	Power- or hand-wash to remove as much chalk as you can before priming.
Clean, unpainted exterior steel	Cold-galvanizing compound	Do not topcoat with alkyd paint.
Rusty, dirty exterior steel	Exterior alkyd primer	Clean and remove loose rust before priming.
Exterior, interior concrete and masonry	Exterior acrylic primer with pigment or acrylic masonry treatment	Sweep to remove loose debris and dust; acid-etch surface if it's greasy or stained.
INTERIOR		
Interior water stains on ceilings, walls	Shellac-based or alkyd sealer	Aerosol spray is especially handy for quick repairs.

>>>

SURFACE	WHAT TO USE	FOR BEST RESULTS
INTERIOR		
Interior surfaces with odor problems	Interior alkyd primer	Clean surfaces and let dry before proceeding.
Unpainted drywall	Interior acrylic primer	Remove drywall sanding dust before priming.
Unpainted interior wood trim	Interior acrylic or alkyd primer	Check compatibility of product when used under enamel.

1:18 BAG IT:

You're ready to put on the colored top coat and you discover that you don't have a tray liner.

⌄

THE QUICK FIX In a pinch, turn to grocery bags. Slip the bag down from the top and smooth it over the well of the tray, then pour the paint in. When you're done, let it dry a bit, pull the bag off, and discard.

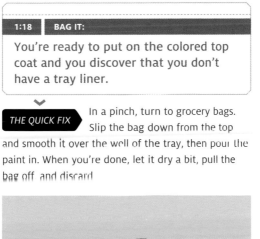

27

> **SAFE AND SOUND:**
> **The Perfect Pail Grip**

Carrying a large pail full of water, paint, or a cleaning mix can be a precarious task. The thin metal handle cuts into your palm making it difficult to keep the pail steady. Make a quick, easy-to-grab handle using a combination open-ended wrench. Position the wrench as a bridge on the inside of the handle and it forms a much sturdier grip for your hand.

Yard Tools

1:19 **TOOL TRACKER:**

For the third time in the afternoon, you can't find the trowel you were just planting annuals with.

THE QUICK FIX Paint wood handles with bright colors or cover rubber handles in brightly colored tape to ensure that garden hand tools are always easy to pick out among the foliage.

You can't seem to keep your garden hose contained.

THE QUICK FIX

Keep the hose coiled in the garage (or outside) around a five-gallon plastic pail. Attach the base of the pail to the wall of the garage with a large-headed nail and wrap the hose around it—it'll spin when you want to pull out the hose—or weight the pail with rocks and hide it standing up between shrubs near the spigot. When the hose is not in use, it's wrapped around the pail. You can store garden supplies inside.

1:21 | **MOWER TRIAGE:**

You need to cut your grass before the in-laws show up but your mower won't start.

THE QUICK FIX Before you give up and take it to the repair shop, try this: Take out the spark plug and empty the gas tank. Install a new plug, add some fresh gas to the tank, and more often than not, the mower will start right up.

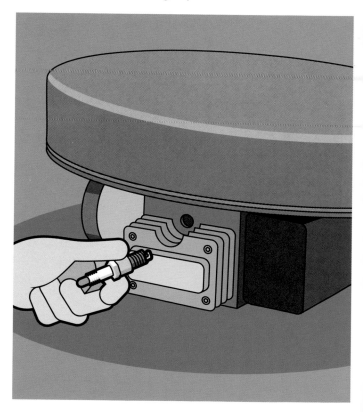

You wait so long to cut your lawn that the mower bogs down as cuttings collect underneath the housing.

THE QUICK FIX   "A smooth, clean deck surface is the best way to keep the mower in top cutting shape," says Clark Oltman, senior service representative for the Toro Company. "Make sure the underside of your deck is clean when you start. Spraying the underside of the housing with cooking spray prior to mowing can be helpful," adds Oltman. You'll maintain your mower better and avoid these chokes if after you've finished mowing, you wipe off all debris with a rag or paper towel, then spray a thin film of light lubricant on the deck surface.

CHAPTER 2:

MAINTENANCE AND CLEANING CLUES

Home maintenance isn't restricted to repairs. In fact, certain tasks—when performed regularly—may actually prevent things from breaking in the first place. But when things do go wrong (and it's inevitable that they do), we have some back-up plans that you can try before you grab the phone to call for pro. Appliances and plumbing are the most frequent offenders, but they also often can be the simplest to care for. From the gutters to the living room carpet, there's a reliable method for keeping every part of your home clean, safe, and well maintained.

MUST-DO MAINTENANCE

The quickest fix is to not have the problem in the first place. Here's a checklist of items every homeowner should get to regularly.

1 > Test your garage door opener monthly to ensure that it reverses when it hits an obstruction or when its sensor beam is interrupted.

2 > Vacuum the clothes dryer's exhaust duct at least once a year. If the duct is plastic, replace it (it's a fire hazard). Rigid sheet-metal ducting is best.

3 > Replace furnace filters quarterly, or as recommended by the furnace manufacturer.

4 > Test all GFCI (ground fault circuit interrupter) outlets monthly. Press the test button and use a voltage tester to make sure the power goes off.

5 > Clean leaves and debris from the condenser of a central air conditioner seasonally.

6 > Once a year, vacuum the refrigerator coils underneath the appliance.

7 > Have the fireplace chimney inspected and cleaned annually.

8 > Inspect window and door caulking and weather stripping yearly.

9 > Replace the batteries in smoke detectors yearly. And remember, even recent hard-wired smoke detectors have backup batteries that must be replaced. If you have never checked yours, do so.

THE QUICK FIX Make gutter cleaning easier—and safer (no ladder required)—with a long spray wand made from a ½-in.-diameter by 10-ft.-long PVC pipe. Cut two 6-in. lengths of pipe. Then use PVC cement to join these short sections and two 90-degree elbows with what is now a 9-ft.-long pipe, forming a J-shaped hook. At the short end of the hook, glue on a solid endcap. Drill three ⅛-in.-diameter holes in the cap. Glue a threaded adapter onto the opposite end of the pipe and attach a garden hose. Place the short end of the J-shaped hook inside the gutter and turn on the hose. As you walk along the house, high-pressure streams of water will rinse the gutter clean.

Clean Heating and Cooling

THE QUICK FIX When baseboard heating is noticeably less efficient than it has been, the cause is often debris on the heating fins responsible for warming air that flows over them. This can happen when you have excessive dust or dirt such as cat hair. You should regularly give the baseboard units a good once-over with a vacuum cleaner or duster to ensure they are heating as efficiently as possible.

35

2:25 **FLUE EPIDEMIC:**

You used to love sitting in front of the fire on a chilly night, but now the smoke gets in your eyes.

THE QUICK FIX If your fireplace has been working fine until recently, the problem is most likely a blockage, caused by an animal's nest or, in unusual cases, a brick or broken piece of flue from the chimney structure. Have a chimney sweep inspect the chimney and remove the obstruction. If the obstruction is creosote buildup, have the chimney professionally swept. Chimneys should be cleaned about once a year, and creosote—a highly flammable carcinogenic—should be removed by a professional.

2:26 **WARMING TREND:**

Your central air-conditioning was working just fine, but suddenly it's cycling on and off and not cooling so well.

THE QUICK FIX The outdoor compressor is designed to stop running under various abnormal situations. One such situation is caused by high internal pressure when obstructions such as leaves, grass clippings, and other debris restrict airflow across the outdoor coil. Check that the fan grill on the unit top and the coil on the unit sides are clear. If the problem is not resolved, turn the air conditioner off to minimize possible damage to the compressor and call a licensed HVAC contractor to have a NATE-certified service technician address the situation.

| 2:27 | **AC DEEP FREEZE:** |

The temperature's jumped from comfortably breezy to a blazing 95 in the shade. You've tripped the switch on your central air, but nothing happens—and the repair service is telling you they can't make it until next week.

THE QUICK FIX It's inevitable that your repair service will be inundated with calls during the first few days of a heat wave. Get a jump on the season and reduce the burden on a system that has been idle for several months. Pat Porzio III, master plumber and electrical contractor, says, "I urge people to test their system as soon as the temperature is in the 70s." Here are the basic steps that Pat advises every homeowner to take at the onset of the cooling season:

+ Change the system's air filter and continue to do so throughout the season at the interval recommended by the manufacturer.
+ As soon as the weather permits, uncover your condenser. Brush or vacuum leaves and grass clippings from it and if it's near the dryer vent, be sure that the condenser's louvers or fins are free of lint.
+ Clean the condensate drain (and pump, if it has one) by pouring in a quart or two of bleach and water solution.
+ Check that all circuit breakers and switches are in the On position.
+ Open all supply vents and return grilles. Move furniture that might be blocking them.
+ Close the humidifier bypass damper, if there is one.
+ And remember, you can maximize battery life by leaving digital thermostats set to Heat or Cool.

With all the above in order, take the system for a test drive. If you hear odd noises, see ice form anywhere, or if the circuit breaker keeps tripping, call for service immediately. Do all this early in the season and you'll be thankful, not sweating.

> KEEP IT CLEAN

Mold and Mildew

2:28   **MOLD BREAKER:**

That pungent smell of bathroom mildew might bring back fond memories of high-school locker rooms and football glory days, but it's not a pretty odor in your house.

THE QUICK FIX   Don't bother with the over-the-counter bathroom leaners—make your own cheaper and more efficient version by mixing about a cup of bleach in a gallon of hot water. Wearing rubber gloves, carefully wash the walls, working from the top down. Let the mixture sit, than rinse the surface well with the hottest water you can get out of the tap (a handheld showerhead works well for this).

2:29   **ROOF GROWTH:**

Mold isn't just a bathroom menace—that green growth on your roof is helping deteriorate the surface

THE QUICK FIX   Remove mold as soon as you notice it—and before it has a chance to form a new roof covering—with a solution of one cup bleach to one gallon warm water. Zinc strips nailed to the roof can prevent mold from returning. Mold grows in dark damp conditions, so cutting back overhanging shade trees can also help alleviate recurring mold problems.

2:30 | **WHITE KNIGHT:**

The grout between the tiles in your bathroom is the color of asphalt.

THE QUICK FIX

Contractors often clean up stained grout lines with a Dremel rotary tool, but you can do a simple fix using hydrogen peroxide and a toothbrush. Saturate the brush in a glass of the peroxide, then dip and scrub to clean the grout lines.

> ### SAFE AND SOUND
> **Recognizing Toxic Mold**
>
> "Toxic" black mold is a serious problem that can cause severe health problems and surface damage that can lead to expensive repairs. The first signs of mold are usually conditions that permit it to flourish. Kevin Roberts, president of the Mold Help Organization, points out that mold needs abundant moisture to grow, so if your part of the country experiences consistently high humidity, you need to be especially watchful. For the same reasons, he suggests keeping an eye out for:
>
> + Recurrent leaks in walls, which leave residual moisture.
>
> + Excessive condensation on pipes that run through confined areas with little air ventilation.
>
> + HVAC systems that experience severe fluctuations in temperature and humidity levels, or HVAC systems that leak.
>
> + A chronically leaky roof.
>
> + Flooding.
>
> If mold has made a home in yours, it's likely the first sign will be a telltale "mildew" odor that doesn't go away. Other signs will be more blatant:
>
> + Cracked or peeling paint on walls.
>
> + Buckling wall surfaces that are moist to the touch.
>
> + Discoloration (especially yellowing or darkening to black) of wall or ceiling surfaces.

- Drywall tape coming loose.

- Chronic and unexplained "allergic" symptoms in members of the household, with no apparent stimuli, or chronic sinus infections.

- Visible mold growth on walls or ceilings.

- Clogged vents or air ducts.

- Cracked or disconnected hoses behind refrigerators from automatic ice makers/water dispensers or dishwashers.

The first step to alleviating a mold problem is assessing its severity, which is often best done by a qualified testing company. Confined cases of mold can often be treated with removal of the affected nonporous area and use of simple treatments such as soap and water. Where the mold is pervasive—such as when it is growing throughout the home's HVAC system or inside of walls—you'll need to use a certified abatement professional. In addition to whatever action is taken to remove the mold, the conditions that caused it to appear in the first place must also be remedied.

> SIDING

Stain Removal

2:31   MERLOT ON THE MARBLE:

You just found out that marble will absorb wine, and now your face isn't the only thing that's red.

THE QUICK FIX   Soak a clean soft cloth in hydrogen peroxide and cover the stain with the cloth. Cover the cloth with a layer of plastic wrap and set a book on top. Keep the cloth on the stain overnight. This will work for any beverage stain.

2:32   A LITTLE OFF THE SIDING:

Your aluminum siding is looking dingy—can you restore its original good looks without replacing it completely?

THE QUICK FIX   If the siding isn't too far gone, then all it might need is a thorough cleaning. To minimize streaking, wash the siding from the bottom to the top, otherwise, the surface below is cleaned unevenly by streams of solution racing down. Rinse from top to bottom. For manual cleaning, use a solution of ⅓ cup non-ammonia detergent, ⅔ cup trisodium phosphate (a cleaning agent and degreaser available at most hardware stores in white powder form), 1 quart laundry bleach, and 3 quarts water. Use a sponge or a soft brush and don't scrub too vigorously or you may remove the finish. If you're pressure washing, use a fan-shaped spray at low pressure, liquid—not powdered—cleaner, and no bleach. Incidentally, if your home has vinyl siding, use vinyl floor cleaner and a large sponge for cleaning.

Subset of Murphy's Law: Only when you're ready to set the table for that really special dinner party will you discover your silverware is tarnished.

THE QUICK FIX Don't bother with the polishing rag—it's a waste of time. Line a disposable lasagna pan with aluminum foil, shiny side up. Fill with enough water to cover your silverware in the pan, add a tablespoon of baking soda and your silverware. Place on a stove burner over low heat for 20 to 30 minutes and the tarnish will transfer to the aluminum foil. However—don't use this method with antique silver pieces; it will strip the black oxidation that gives the detail on those pieces their character.

2:34   **LIKE NEW:**

Nothing says "sad home" like rust stains in your bathtub.

THE QUICK FIX   Although long-term rust stains may be a sign that the tub needs to be refinished or replaced, oxidation stains of a more recent vintage can be removed with a paste made of hydrogen peroxide and cream of tartar. Scrub the paste in and leave it for a few minutes, then rinse thoroughly with hot water to remove it. Repeat as necessary.

2:35   **GLUE CLUE:**

Crafts accident! The balsa wood plane is in one piece, but your living room couch has a nice dab of white glue front and center.

THE QUICK FIX   If you have kids or crafters in your home, this is going to be a frequent ocurrence. Luckily, you most likely have everything needed for removal at hand. Use a dull straightedge, such as a spatula or letter opener, to remove whatever glue you can without spreading it out. Then, according to Mary Ellen, star of HGTV's *TIPical Mary Ellen* and author of *It Works! Over a Thousand New Uses for Common Household Items*, "Combine a mixture of one part warm water to one part white vinegar in a spray bottle and moisten the stain area and blot off the glue. Repeat as necessary, and rinse with cool water when the stain is gone. Dry with a clean, absorbent cloth."

2:36 **A LASTING IMPRESSION:**

You've rearranged the living room furniture but the carpet still shows depressions from where the sofa used to be.

THE QUICK FIX Use a steam iron to remove carpet indentations. Hold the iron over the depression and apply steam. Don't press the iron down on the carpet—just saturate the area with steam, then rake the fibers with your fingers. Depending on how old and deep the depression is, it may be necessary to steam the area several times to remove it.

2:37 | **DISTURBING EVIDENCE:**

Unless it's a crime scene, you should remove a blood-stain in carpeting as soon as possible.

THE QUICK FIX Blot the stain as much as possible, using a paper towel. Mix a teaspoon of household ammonia into a quart of cold water and dab the stain with a paper towel soaked in this solution, trying not to moisten the carpet backing. Combine a squirt of dish soap with a quart of water and use a new paper towel soaked in this mixture to continue dabbing the stain until it is removed. Moisten the area with a paper towel that has been soaked with cold water, and dab to remove all remaining residue.

2:38 | **CHEERS AND TEARS:**

A marvelous cocktail party is cause for alarm when red wine spills right in the middle of your new beige wall-to-wall.

THE QUICK FIX The secret to removing wine spills is to act quickly. Neutralize the stain with a small amount of white wine, then pour a little salt over the stain to stop it from setting into the carpet fiber. Once the salt absorbs the wine, suck it up with a dustbuster or blot with a paper towel. Sprinkle with club soda and blot immediately. Repeat the process as necessary to get all the wine out.

2:39 | **PET POTTY FLOOR:**

You're late getting home and Fido just couldn't wait.

THE QUICK FIX Clean up the accident as soon as possible. Then follow these directions, courtesy of Steve Seabaugh, technical director for the National Wood Flooring Association. "If the floor is finished with a surface finish (either water-based or oil-based), use a five-percent phenol solution—available from any hardware store—to clean the area thoroughly, using a damp, soft cloth. Stains and odor are caused by bacteria, and the phenol solution will kill the bacteria before it has a chance to damage your floor. If the floor is finished with a wax finish, use #000 fine steel wool and a small amount of mineral spirits to clean the area, rubbing gently in a circular motion, then wax and buff the area."

2:40 — THE WRONG SCUFF:

Your nice pair of wingtips just marred the surface of your pristine vinyl kitchen floor.

THE QUICK FIX Use a soft cloth soaked in mineral spirits to remove the scuff. Test under the refrigerator or in some out-of-the-way location to ensure the spirits won't discolor your particular brand of flooring.

Bad Buildup

2:41 — CRUST BUSTER:

It's perfect weather for a nice barbecue, but first you have to get that rocklike coating off the grill.

THE QUICK FIX Remove loose debris from the grill, then make a paste out of baking soda and water. Scrub the paste onto the grill and let sit for an hour. Wash off the paste with a hose, rinsing thoroughly, and then fire up the grill to remove any leftover residue.

2:42 — HORROR FILM:

Baked on crud makes the inside of your microwave look like a food-fight victim, and the smell is no treat for the nose.

THE QUICK FIX Put a glass bowl filled with a half-and-half mixture of water and white vinegar into the microwave and run on high for about three minutes. Then wipe down the inside. You can also deodorize the interior by leaving a bowl of vinegar sitting inside overnight.

You haven't used your dishwasher for a couple of weeks and now it smells funky and looks dingy.

THE QUICK FIX Odd as it seems, because of the constant moisture in the dishwasher and the fact that a lot of organic matter makes its way around the inside, the interior of a dishwasher can easily become a grungy place; especially if the unit sits unused for a significant period of time. Bring it back to cleanliness by running the dishwasher empty, with a cup of bleach in a mug or bowl on the lower shelf (make sure you have no soap in the soap dispenser or anywhere else in the unit). Then run the dishwasher again, adding lemon juice that has been frozen into ice cubes or a packet of powdered lemonade mix, placed in the soap dish and silverware container. Run it one last time and the dishwasher should be fresh and ready for dishes.

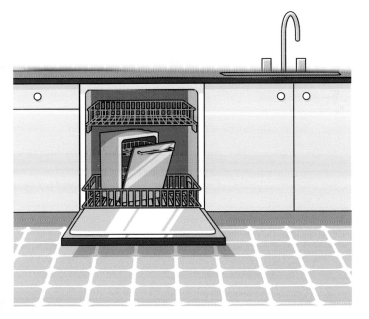

2:44 **WALL OF SHAME:**

Soap scum and mineral buildup have turned your glass shower doors into a solid wall of yuck.

THE QUICK FIX When cleaning water deposits, turn to the magic of fabric-softening sheets, the type you throw in the dryer to keep your clothes soft. These are imbued with chemicals that soften water deposits, whether they are trapped in fabric or crusted on your shower door. Scrub the doors with a scrub brush to loosen any deposits, then wipe with a handful of the sheets.

2:45 **CLEAN CUT:**

Looking to block harmful UV rays and prevent furniture fading, the previous owners of your house put protective film on key windows. But time has taken its toll and the film is scratched, discolored, and ugly.

THE QUICK FIX Joe Richard, Technical Marketing Engineer for CP Films, Inc., says that the technique for removing the film depends on what type of film it is. "Film that was applied with clear distortion-free (CDF) adhesive will have to be removed using a razor scraper with stainless-steel blades, keeping the film wet with a soapy water solution. Window film applied with PS adhesive (tacky to the touch) can be removed with a cleaning solution made by filling a liter bottle with ⅓ sudsy ammonia and ⅔ water. When the window has been in direct sunlight for at least an hour, spray the film side liberally with the mixture. Cover the surface with clear plastic wrap and be sure your room is well ventilated. After an hour, leave the wrap in place and use a razor blade to lift a corner of the film. If you're careful, you should be able to slowly pull away the film and adhesive cleanly in one piece or several large pieces. Any residual adhesive should be sprayed with soapy water and the pane scraped clean with a razor."

2:46 | **UNSTICK TRICK:**

You're finally ready to redo your kitchen cabinets, but you face deteriorating contact paper on the shelves.

THE QUICK FIX — Use an iron on low heat to warm the paper until it comes up from the shelf surface, then remove the remaining glue with isopropyl alcohol and a scraper.

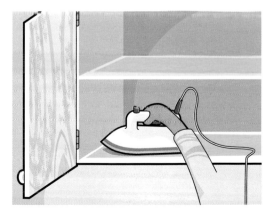

2:47	HOLD THE LIME:

The lime buildup on your faucets and fixtures needs to be taken care of not only because it's unsightly but because it leads to corrosion.

THE QUICK FIX The way to beat lime, an alkaline mineral deposit, is with an acidic material. You can try lemon juice—not only natural but leaves a nice scent—but one of the best is white vinegar warmed up in the microwave. Soak a paper towel or rag and leave on the area for 10 to 15 minutes. Use the towel to wipe the lime deposits off, then rinse the area well with clean, cold water. If that doesn't work, a hardware-store product called CLR (calcium, lime, rust) will certainly remove the deposits.

> **SAFE AND SOUND:**
> **Alleviating Lead Paint**
>
> If your home is more than 30 years old, the chances are good that lead paint was used in it. If you suspect you have lead paint, you should test with a home test kit or hire a professional inspector. Wherever lead paint has been used, repairs—even quick fixes—can pose a significant hazard of releasing lead into the home environment. Any abrading of a wall surface with lead paint may create toxic dust and chips that are especially dangerous to children. You can choose to encapsulate lead-paint surfaces with special coatings that bond the paint, ensuring it won't contaminate the home, or you can remove it with special strippers that saturate the paint and allow you to strip it off whole. But a lead-abatement professional is the way to go if the paint is chipping and already causing a hazard.

2:48 | **POISON PERFUME:**

Drain odors are making your kitchen an unpleasant place in which to spend time.

THE QUICK FIX

Pour a cup of white vinegar down the drain, let it stand for 30 minutes, then rinse with hot water.

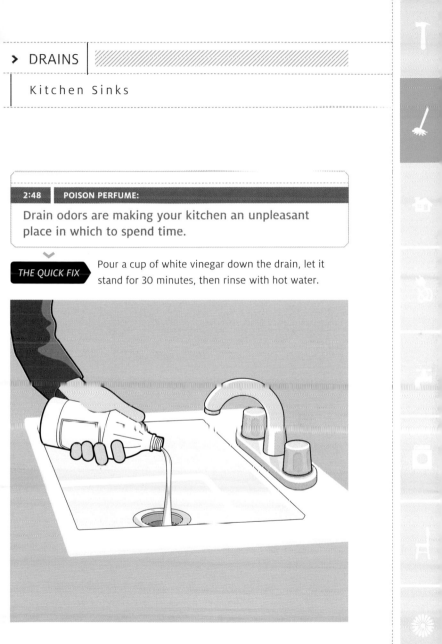

2:49 | **SLIME TIME:**

You're right in the middle of preparing that big Thanksgiving feast, when your kitchen sink chokes on all the grease that you've been allowing to go down the drain.

THE QUICK FIX Use a heating pad wrapped around the drain trap (or a hair dryer if you're willing to hold it there) until the metal becomes hot. This will melt the grease and allow you to flush it away with a running stream of hot water.

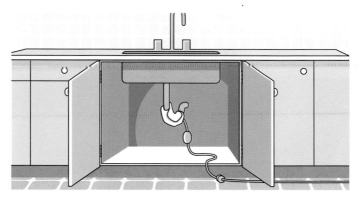

2:50 | **SMELL HOLE:**

The odors wafting out of your garbage disposal are more fitting for a sewer than a kitchen sink.

THE QUICK FIX Disposals can retain food bacteria in the blades, making for an olfactory nightmare. Clean out the unit with a cup of white vinegar followed by a flush of very hot water.

2:51 | **SLOW MOTION:**

Your bathroom sink is draining little
but your patience.

THE QUICK FIX The handy plunger is one of the
best tools for a slow-moving drain.
Fill the sink with a few inches of water to provide a
good seal around the plunger. Next, stuff a wet rag
into the overflow opening of the sink. Try to completely fill the opening so that you get a good seal. By
blocking the opening, no air can reach the drain,
which greatly increases the effectiveness of the
plunger. Finally, plunge away.

> ### DISASTER PREVENTION:
> **5 Simple Steps to Prevent Drain Clogs**
>
> Stopping clogs is a battle fought on two fronts. First, you should be careful about what goes down the drain. Second, you need to take regular action to clear small deposits that inevitably form in any drain.
>
> 1 > Use drain screens to keep hair, soap scum, and other solids from making their way into the drain.
>
> 2 > Never pour grease down the drain, and clean greasy pots and pans as thoroughly as possible with a paper towel before cleaning in hot water in the sink.
>
> 3 > Never dump chemicals such as paint or paint thinners down a drain—even a shower drain or utility sink.
>
> 4 > Clean all your sink stoppers regularly.
>
> 5 > Once a week (make it a regular part of your weekly cleaning schedule) pour boiling hot water down your drains.

2:52 | **CLEAN OUT:**

Your drain won't—and the plunger you have isn't strong enough.

THE QUICK FIX — In an emergency, you can use a wet/dry shop vacuum to help clear a clog. Put the mouth of the vacuum hose over the drain opening and seal around it with a wet cloth (also plug up any overflow holes). Turn the vacuum on and off quickly until the clog clears.

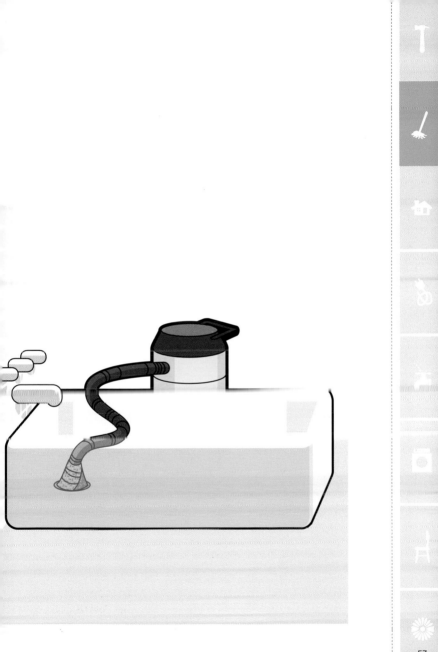

2:53 | **STANDING WATER:**

Soap scum and the residue of other body and hair products have packed your shower drain to capacity.

THE QUICK FIX If simple plunging, hot water, or chemical drain cleaners don't work, you may need a more powerful ally.

Run a garden hose in through a nearby window and secure it in the opening of the drain (drying the shower floor thoroughly and duct taping the hose securely in place is a good option). Once you're certain the hose has been sealed in the drain, turn on the spigot full force and it should blast the clog free.

> **SAFE AND SOUND:**
> **Dangerous Additions: How Not to Unclog a Toilet**
>
> Trust us, nobody likes to plunge a toilet. But the frustration that comes from having a clog can lead to some inadvisable home remedies. Never put boiling water down a toilet. Although it seems like this might break up a clog, the water in your toilet is cold (in winter, it may be very cold) and the difference in temperature can lead to damage to your toilet or pipes. If for any reason you put bleach into the toilet, do not combine it with any other cleaner or chemical clog remover. The combination could create deadly chlorine gas. For most toilet clogs, the best answer is usually a mechanical one, such as a snake or—sadly—the old-time plunger.

Basements

2:54 **UNPLANNED POOL:**

A big rain has flooded your basement. And since it knocked out the power too, your usually reliable sump pump won't pump.

THE QUICK FIX If you live on a slope, try making a siphon. First, fill a garden hose with water from the outside spigot. Seal one end with your thumb and have a friend seal the other. Place one end through the cellar window and into the standing water. Then, have your friend carry the other end as far downhill as possible (the outlet has to be below the intake). Release your thumbs and let gravity do the rest.

2:55 **TRAPPED BELOW:**

The water in the trap of your basement-floor drain dried up, and now your cellar smells vaguely of nasty, nasty things.

THE QUICK FIX Pour nontoxic plumbing antifreeze down the drain to fill the trap. You can use water in a pinch, but it evaporates faster than antifreeze, so you'll need to repeat the process more often. If you have pets in your home, make sure to block access to the area.

CHAPTER 3:

STRUCTURAL QUANDARIES

In the home—as in life—

it's often the little things that matter. And it's amazing how many small structural things can go wrong around your house. Whether it's the front-door lock that won't let you into your own home, or the cracked window that won't keep the cold out, small household problems can have a big effect. For most of these, there's no need to call for a repair-man—the solution lies in tapping your ingenuity and using a few common house-hold materials in innovative ways. Even when it seems that the roof is falling in—or the floor is opening up beneath you—there are often simple ways to solve larger problems on your own.

> DOORS, WINDOWS AND LOCKS

Doors

3:56 | STICKY SITUATION:

The bedroom door sticks every time it's opened or closed, but the idea of repeatedly hanging and planing or sanding what you think are the trouble spots seems like more work than it's worth.

THE QUICK FIX Tape carbon paper or another type of blued paper along the edge that is sticking. Open and close the door, and the bluing will mark the problem areas, allowing you to sand or plane exactly the points that are causing the door to stick. This works on the side, top, or bottom.

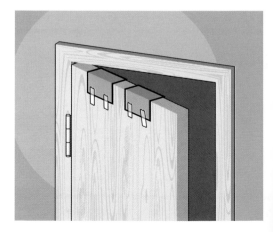

You're starting to think you live in a haunted house because every time you open the door, your entrance is announced by a squeak coming from the hinges.

THE QUICK FIX   Just lifting the hinge pin and squirting a little oil into the hinge will work for the short run, but the squeaking will inevitably return. To ensure long-lasting silence, tap the hinge pin out of the hinge and coat the pin with white lithium grease. Tap the pin back in place and test the door. The door should open and close silently, although you may have to lubricate both top and bottom hinges.

Privacy's at stake when the bathroom door is out of kilter and binds on one corner.

THE QUICK FIX   Close the door and inspect the clearance along the sides and top to see if it's misaligned in the frame. Check the hinge mortises to see if one is deeper than the other. If so, install a thin cardboard shim or playing card under the hinge leave to adjust the alignment. If necessary, add more shims until the door swings freely.

3:59   **ROUGH RIDE:**

A sliding glass door that doesn't stay in its track is more than a minor annoyance, it's a safety hazard.

THE QUICK FIX First, check if the door has adjustable rollers and adjust to improve the door's action. The metal guides that contain most sliding glass doors can get bent out of shape by daily wear and tear. Badly bent or flattened guides will allow the door to slide out of the track and badly damaged tracks need to be reformed into their original shape. Use a scrap piece of lumber (or a large building block from a child's wood block set) that is just thick enough to fit into the slot of the tracks. Secure the wood in place and use a mallet to pound the track guides back into their correct position.

Every house has one, a door that slowly drifts shut every time you try to leave it open.

THE QUICK FIX Rather than resetting the hinges or propping it open with a potted plant, remove one of the hinge pins, lay it on a hard surface, and strike it lightly with a hammer until the hinge pin has a slight bend. Tap the pin back in place. The increased friction will keep the door where you want it.

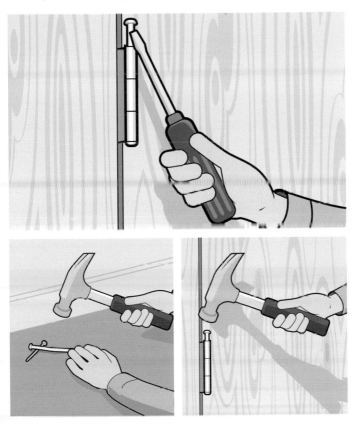

Windows

3:61 **CRACKING UP:**

Your son's backyard pitching session got a little wild, now you need a temporary patch to keep the chill out until you get time to replace a shattered window pane.

THE QUICK FIX Wear heavy-duty work gloves to remove the broken glass, then staple a square of thick plastic (a double thickness of a heavy-duty garbage bag works well) onto the surrounding sash or mullions.

3:62 | TAPPING SESSION:

The stresses and strains in your old double-hung windows have caused a crack, but it will be days before you can get to the hardware store for a new pane.

THE QUICK FIX Keep rain and wind on the right side of the window by applying masking tape firmly to both sides of the crack.

3:63 | GRAND OPENING:

With the painting finished, you want a little cross breeze of fresh air in the room, but it seems the window sash has been painted shut.

THE QUICK FIX Run a utility knife between the sash and stop to break the paint bond (you may have to do this more than once). If paint has seeped deep into the joint between the two pieces, you'll need to extend the blade of a utility knife and slide it all the way in between.

3:64   OPEN SEASON:

Those handsome wood double-hung windows absorb the summer humidity like a sponge, and now they're so swollen they're sticking.

THE QUICK FIX Mayan Metzler, president of MyHome Certified Remodeling Specialists in New York City, suggests starting with a hair dryer. "Blow hot air around the edge of the sash until you can move the window. Once it moves, lubricate the channel guides (the wood strips that create the groove in which the sash travels) with an unscented white votive candle (best because it's essentially pure paraffin) or candle wax." Metzler adds, "If the problem persists, use a mallet and a small, square block of wood to lightly tap the channel guides outward, slightly enlarging the channel."

The neighbor kid just got a high-powered BB gun for his birthday, and now you have to fix a perfect little hole in your window.

THE QUICK FIX To the cosmetics case! Carefully dab a bit of clear nail polish into the hole. Wait until it dries, and repeat until you've built up the nail polish flush with the window surface. If you've done a good job, the hole will be invisible and you may not need to replace the pane at all.

> **SAFE AND SOUND:**
> **Working with Stuck or Broken Windows**
>
> It's the nature of window glass that it breaks into sharp shards. Therefore, never rush when dealing with a window problem and never bang on a stuck window sash or pane because you could easily slip and put your hand right through the glass. Take your time when removing glass shards and don't try to jerk them free. Always wear thick leather or other puncture-proof work gloves. Use duct tape to pick up shards that have fallen out of the window, and wrap the edges of shards still in the window with the tape before you remove the pieces. If the pieces seem firmly affixed in the sash, brush the putty with linseed oil and let sit for a few hours. This may soften the putty and make it easier and less risky to remove the shards. Otherwise you will need to carefully remove the dried putty with a wood chisel.

3:66 MESH PATCH:

A small rip in a window screen is like a neon sign inviting flies to come on in.

THE QUICK FIX Cut a square of fabric from a torn pair of nylon pantyhose or stockings. The square should be slightly larger than the hole or tear in the screen. Run a bead of superglue or other clear cyanoacrylate adhesive around the edge of the patch and gently place it over the perforation in the window screen, holding it there for a minute or two to let the glue set.

Locks

3:67 LOCK MESS MONSTER:

You try to open your front door but the key sticks as if you were pushing it into a wad of chewing gum.

THE QUICK FIX Over time, lock tumblers can become misaligned and clogged with all kinds of gunk. The way to ensure your key makes a clean entrance and exit every time is by providing effective lubrication that won't add to the gunk. The best is powdered graphite. Also check frequently used keys for roughened edges. Gently and carefully use a nail file to smooth burrs off the key tip.

3:68 COLD WAR:

Anyone who has lived in a cold climate knows that frozen locks go with the territory.

THE QUICK FIX According to David Lowell, CML, CMST, and Director of Training and Certification for the Associated Locksmiths of America, it's a matter of bringing the heat. "If the lock to your house is iced over, remove the ice from the opening of the lock cylinder and carefully heat the key with a match or lighter. If you don't have a match or lighter, place the key on your car's engine block or radiator until it's very hot. Holding the key with your gloves on to avoid burning your fingers, insert the key into the lock and work it gently back and forth until the ice melts and the cylinder turns."

3:69 SAFETY'S SAKE:

The lock on your sliding glass door (if it exists at all) is about as substantial a theft deterrent as a picture of a guard dog.

 THE QUICK FIX Cut down a broomstick or mop handle to fit snuggly in the floor channel in which the doors slide open or closed. When in the channel, the stick will jam and prevent anyone from opening the doors.

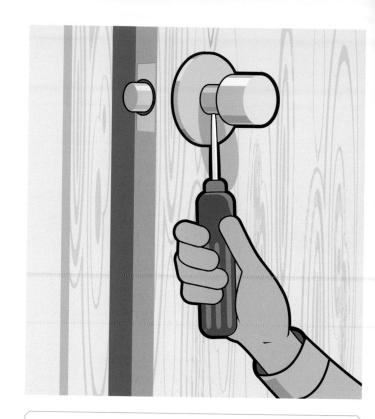

3:70 | **HIDDEN FEATURE:**

You're ready to remove a defective lockset, but how you begin to get it the darn thing off the door is a major mystery.

THE QUICK FIX For the sake of aesthetics, most standard locksets (those with doorknobs, not handles) mount the knob with hidden screws, making it appear as if there is no way to remove them short of a crowbar and large hammer. But save yourself the cost of a new door. If you look underneath on the stem of the knob itself, you'll find a tiny hole. Just insert a small pry tool, such as a thin straight screwdriver, and pull on the knob to remove it. Work the faceplate off and the mounting hardware will be accessible underneath.

> **FIX OR DITCH?**
> **The Case for a New Lockset**

A lockset is the mechanism by which you open and secure a door. Despite the name, locksets may not require a key. Privacy locks, usually used for bathrooms or bedrooms, may have a simple turn or push-button lock.

There are three basic reasons for replacing a lockset. In some cases, the lockset is malfunctioning and may have failed. More commonly, homeowners look to upgrade from, say, a common "passage" lockset to a key-operated lockset. Changing locksets may also be a function of aesthetics, as homeowners change the style of their doors and other accessories and accents.

According to Tom Embriani of Black & Decker Hardware and Home Improvement Group, "Most modest locksets can be repaired with minimal effort and expertise, but older units may require replacement because parts are no longer available to repair them. Signs that you should replace a lockset include a lock that operates intermittently or requires multiple attempts to get it to lock, or a clunking or grinding noise along with a looseness in the cylinder (where you insert your key). If the lock simply refuses to turn, or the knob spins freely, components in the lockset are worn out or defective and it should be repaired or replaced."

3:71 — CRACKED TEETH:

Someone—not you, surely—has broken a key off in a door lock, which is now jammed shut.

THE QUICK FIX Use a grinding wheel to shape an old hacksaw blade into a harpoonlike point. Then, slip the point into the lock over one of the key nubs and use the hook to fish it out.

3:72 — NUMBER CRUNCHER:

You're in a hurry to get to tennis class when you realize that you've forgotten the combination for your locker's combination lock.

THE QUICK FIX If your lock is of fairly recent vintage you're in luck. Chances are the manufacturer has the combination on file, keyed to the code number on the lock. Visit the manufacturer's website and you're likely to find a FAQ section dealing with recovering lost combinations. Some manufacturers even offer online registration so that if you do forget the combination, you can easily retrieve it.

You've finally set aside an afternoon to clear out that storage shed that hasn't seen the light of day in a year. But now you discover the padlock is rusted shut.

THE QUICK FIX   Immerse the lock in kerosene or penetrating lubricant for 24 hours. If the lock is attached to the hasp of a garage, gate, or other structure, this will mean wiring a metal can full of kerosene to the structure to allow the lock to soak in place.

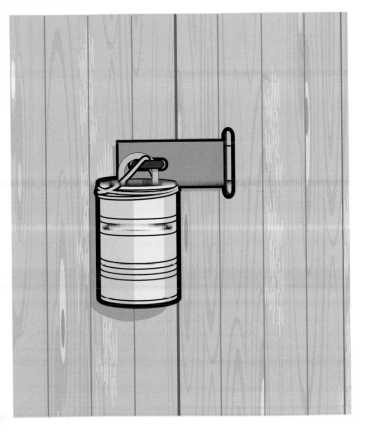

> WALLS AND FLOORS

Walls

3:74 | **PATCH PERFECT:**

A little roughhousing seemed harmless enough until someone's elbow found its way through the drywall.

THE QUICK FIX Cover the hole with a peel-and-stick drywall repair screen. If you can't find one at your local hardware store, try this: Use a wallboard saw or utility knife to cut a square around the hole. Insert a short piece of scrap wood as a brace, holding it against the back side of the wall, while you insert screws into it from the front. Cut a drywall patch using the square you removed as a template. Coat the back of the patch with compound and press into place against the brace. Now tape and compound the patch and paint to match the rest of the wall.

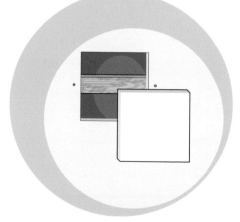

Hairline cracks in your living room wall are driving you crazy as they come back months after you've spackled, sanded, and painted.

THE QUICK FIX First, widen the crack slightly by scraping with the pointed end of a can opener. Remove all dust and cover the crack with 2-in.-wide adhesive-backed fiberglass mesh drywall tape. Cut the tape if necessary to follow the crack, but don't overlap pieces. Use a drywall knife to apply a thin coat of joint compound over the tape. The next day, sand lightly and follow with two wider, thinner coats of compound.

A large bubble in wallpaper sticks out like a sore thumb.

THE QUICK FIX Cut an X in the bubble using a utility knife with a new blade. Peel back the edges of the cut wallpaper and carefully apply wallpaper adhesive. Smooth down the edges so that the cut lines are blended in and disappear.

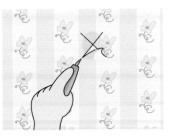

3:77 | **FISSURE FIX:**

A split in wood siding isn't just unsightly, it's an open highway for water and other elements to get in and damage your walls.

THE QUICK FIX Vince Butler, president of Butler Brothers Corporation in Clifton, Virginia, and chair of the National Association of Home Builders Remodelers Council, suggests a way to avoid the expense and effort of replacing the entire board. "Wedge a small shim under the siding board until the bottom half of the split is exposed, then coat the exposed edge of the split with a high-quality waterproof wood glue. Use a syringe to apply the glue as deep into the crack as possible." Then it's just a matter of ensuring the split dries tight. "It's best to wedge or clamp the board if you can, but if not, you should nail the board above and below the split, predrilling for the nails. Cover the nails with wood putty; sand and repaint the siding board to match."

CRUMBLE CURE

Plaster walls have a way of coming apart with little prompting. Make sure your walls don't go to pieces when hanging a mirror or picture by making a small pilot hole that is slightly smaller than the nail. The drill bit must be long enough to penetrate completely through the plaster and the lath behind it. When in doubt, use a screw instead of a nail to spare brittle plaster walls the force of impact.

Bathrooms

3:78 BLEMISH BAN:

That wood table was heavier than you thought, and dragging it across the room has left a nice long abrasion in your pretty wood floor.

THE QUICK FIX According to Rusty Swindoll, assistant technical director with the National Wood Flooring Association, the fix depends on the type of floor. "If the floor is finished with wax, fine surface scratches can be concealed with a liberal amount of wood-floor paste wax, rubbed in with the grain using a fine-grain steel wool pad. Remove the excess wax and buff the surface lightly with a cloth." But, he adds, "If the floor is finished with a surface finish (either water- or oil-based), use the meat from a pecan or walnut that has been crushed, rubbing it over the surface scratches to camouflage the scratch."

3:79 HEALING THE FLOOR:

The last thing you need in a busy kitchen is another tripping hazard, which is exactly what that blister in your resilient flooring has become.

THE QUICK FIX Puncture the blister with a sharp prick such as a small nail and use a glue syringe to shoot flooring adhesive under the surface of the blister. Cover the blister with several heavy bricks or other weight and leave for 24 hours or until the epoxy is fully cured.

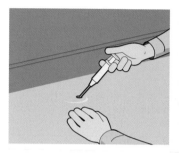

3:80 SHARING SQUARES:

You just learned the hard way that dragging a heavy metal garbage pail can ruin a vinyl kitchen tile.

THE QUICK FIX Ideally, you thought ahead when the floor was installed and put aside a few extra tiles. If not, you can scavenge a replacement tile from underneath the refrigerator or stove (this will be harder if the tiles are light colored because the floor will be more faded than the replacement tile). Remove the old tile by heating it with an iron set on low until you can pry it up with a putty knife. Remove the warm adhesive, apply new adhesive, and lay down the replacement tile. Weight it down with bricks or other heavy objects until the adhesive cures.

Every home seems to have that one area of wood floor that squeaks, and yours is driving you to distraction.

THE QUICK FIX Squeaks almost always occur in the subfloor, not the wood floor itself, according to Ed Korczak, executive director with the National Wood Flooring Association. "The best solution is to secure the subfloor from below by driving screws into the subfloor of the area that is squeaking. Be sure the screws are short enough so that they don't break the surface of the face of the wood floor."

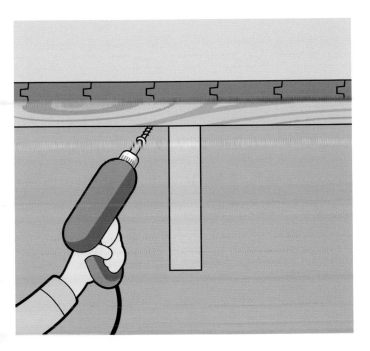

3:82 **SCAR TISSUE:**

Your resilient flooring isn't resilient to small scratches and scuffs.

THE QUICK FIX Rub the scratch with the edge of a quarter. If the blemish is still apparent, rub a tiny amount of paste wax on the surface and buff it with a clean soft cloth.

3:83 **SQUARE SHOOTER:**

So now you know: Dropping a cast-iron pan really will crack a ceramic tile.

THE QUICK FIX Remove the grout around the tile carefully using a grout saw (this is not a mechanical saw but a simple abrasive tool that you run along grout lines). Then chip out the tile with a small cold chisel. Once you've removed all the tile pieces, try to remove as much as possible of the existing adhesive left over from the tile. Lay down a bed of new adhesive and press the new tile in place. Grout around the tile and let sit for 24 hours before walking on it.

SLOW BURN:

Uncle Bill finally went home, taking his stinking stogie with him, but he left behind a nice burn mark in your carpet.

THE QUICK FIX First, discreetly clip away damaged fibers with a sharp pair of scissors, then lightly scrub with a scouring pad to remove the darkened tips of the carpet fibers. Vacuum to remove the singed particles. For deeper or more serious burns, you'll need to patch the carpet. Unless you have a leftover remnant from when the carpet was installed, this will mean finding an area of carpet that is rarely seen—such as in a closet or underneath a piece of furniture—and removing a patch. Use a utility knife and jar lid to cut a neat circle around the burn mark, and cut an identical circle out of the donor carpet section. Use double-edged tape or carpet adhesive to set the patch firmly in place.

> MISCELLANEOUS SMALL REPAIRS

3:85 **HOLDING ON:**

That wobbly staircase handrail is a law-suit waiting to happen.

THE QUICK FIX A handrail is only as good as its main support—known as the newel post—the thick post positioned where the handrail begins at the bottom of the stairs. Don Sever of Sever Construction in Oakton, Virginia, recommends a simple solution: "Stabilize the handrail by securing the newel post more firmly to its base. Drill a hole near the bottom of the post, using a 1-in. spade bit, drilling into the foundation of the staircase frame. Drill a ⅜-in. hole in the center of the larger hole, through the post into a framing member. Now ratchet a ½-in. x 5-in. wood screw into the hole until the fit is tight. Bore a smaller countersunk hole above the first hole and in line with the center of the bottom stair tread, and screw in a number 12 x 4 in. wood screw. This smaller screw insures against splitting the stair tread. Conceal both screws with a wood plug."

3:86 **FLOPPY BACKSPLASH:**

Your kitchen backsplash has pulled away from the wall, and you're concerned about water dripping down behind the counter.

THE QUICK FIX Many kitchen backsplashes aren't nailed or screwed to the counter-top, but glued to the wall—and, in time, they can pull free. To reattach a loose backsplash, first use a putty knife to scrape off old glue. Apply two beads of construction adhesive to the rear of the backsplash, and a bead of clear silicone sealant along its bottom edge. Set the backsplash in position and press it against the wall and counter. To hold the backsplash while the adhesive cures, wedge 1-in. x 2-in. strips diagonally between the top edge of the backsplash and the underside of the upper kitchen wall cabinet.

3:87   OVER THE EDGE:

You never think about countertop edging until it comes loose and gets in the way of your cooking.

THE QUICK FIX Use a putty knife to scrape out all loose dried adhesive. Then use a nail or screw to hold the flap away from the countertop, and liberally apply contact cement to the inside of the flap and the edge of the countertop, making sure to keep away from the top and bottom edges to prevent excess glue from squeezing out. Tighten a C-clamp at the damaged area. Use pieces of wood under the clamp's jaws to prevent marring the surface. Then, insert two tapered wood shims from opposite directions between the clamp and the edging. Tap in the shims to hold the edge in place while the glue dries.

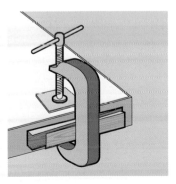

3:88 | **HOLD THE STARCH:**

You've just dropped your hammer on a piece of carefully prepared stock, leaving an unsightly dent.

THE QUICK FIX After you've finished groaning and swearing, it's relatively easy to fix the problem. Place a few drops of clean water in the dent and allow it to soak in for about a minute. Place a clean cotton cloth over the dent and use a household iron, on a medium-high setting, to heat the dent. The steam will cause the crushed wood fibers to swell, bringing the dented area flush to the surrounding material. You may have to repeat the procedure two or three times for a stubborn dent. The steam will raise the wood grain, so you will need to sand the surface once the dent is gone.

3:89 | **MITER MEND:**

The small gaps in your baseboard corners are big eyesores.

THE QUICK FIX Gaps in joints are usually caused by a general settling of the house. To fix the gaps in the traditional way would require removing and recutting the molding. But save the effort with a little simple cosmetic surgery; simply rub the round shaft of a screwdriver along the joint on each side with a light pressure, until the wood compresses to close the gap.

That bent metal closet rod is going to come down sooner or later—most likely when you're late for work and need to get dressed in a hurry.

THE QUICK FIX Unscrew and remove the rod from its mountings in the closet. Measure the inside diameter of the rod and purchase a wooden dowel of the next smaller diameter (available at home centers and hardware stores)—sometimes a broomstick will work as well. Cut the wooden rod slightly shorter than the closet rod, and insert it inside the metal tube, straightening the metal as you go. Reinstall the rod and you're back in business.

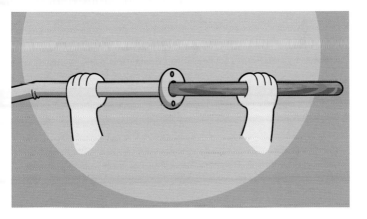

> UP ON THE ROOF

3:91 SHINGLES BAR:

A bad storm has damaged a shingle on your roof; you need to protect the roof from further damage by way of the compromised shingle.

 THE QUICK FIX

Gather a tube of roofing cement and a piece of aluminum flashing (available at home centers). Cut the flashing about 1 inch narrower than the ripped tab and about 4 inches longer so that it extends under the tabs on either side. Use a flat pry bar to carefully loosen the damaged tab and the tabs to the left and right. Next, apply two or three thick beads of roofing cement to the surface beneath the shingle. Slip the flashing underneath and apply more roofing cement on top of the flashing. Press the tab down to adhere the flashing to the roof.

3:92 A SHINGLE SWITCH:

A few of your wooden shingles have become split and you need to replace them.

 THE QUICK FIX

A typical wood-shingle house is covered with thousands of individual shingles and, over time, it's inevitable that a few will split or become damaged. To replace a single shingle, first use a chisel and hammer to split it into several narrow pieces, then yank them out with pliers. Slip a hacksaw blade under the shingle above and cut through the nails that held the old shingle in place. Next, use a utility knife to trim a new shingle to match the width of the space. Slide the shingle in place and tap it to within 1 inch of its final position. Drive in two galvanized cedar shingle nails at an upward angle, directly below the butt edge of the shingle above. Then use a wood block and hammer to tap the new shingle up into place. As the shingle slides in place, it'll pull the nailheads up and behind the shingle above.

> **GO WITH THE PRO:**
> **Assessing a Roof Leak**

Some overhead leaks are due to minor problems—such as a single torn shingle or a small hole in flashing—that you can usually handle with a little DIY experience and some basic tools. But other situations call for a roofer's expertise. If you can't fix the problem quickly and completely, call a pro in as soon as possible; water damage spreads quickly, even from a small leak. A licensed roofer is best when

1 > There are multiple leaks.

2 > The leak is wicking across framing members or along walls, making it difficult for you to trace the actual source.

3 > A repair you made is not holding.

4 > The leak entails significant damage to roofing surface or flashed areas.

5 > The roof surface, such as ceramic tile roof, is beyond your abilities.

3:93   CHIMNEY SEEP:

No matter what you do, the paint on your chimney masonry keeps peeling.

THE QUICK FIX Install a galvanized (good), stainless (better), or copper (best) rain cap. These start at about $30 and are available in most home-repair and building-supply outlets. "Peeling chimney paint is almost always caused by water working its way from the inside out," explains John Stauffer, technical director at the Paint Quality Institute. "A rain cap will keep the bulk of the water out of the flue."

SAFE AND SOUND
Avoiding the Freefall

Working on a roof is obviously a dangerous under-taking. But some simple safety measures can ensure that you don't take the quick way down.

+ To minimize the possibility of a slip and to prevent damage to the roof, step on the roof as little as possible.

+ If you are going to do extensive work on the roof, buy or rent a roofer's ladder with a bracket that bridges the ridge of the roof.

+ When on the roof, use a strong safety harness or belt secured by a lifeline attached to a stable fixture such as the base of a chimney.

+ Access the roof by way of a high-quality extension ladder, secured to the house in at least two places.

+ Never work on a roof in icy conditions. Dark-colored shingles can hide ice patches.

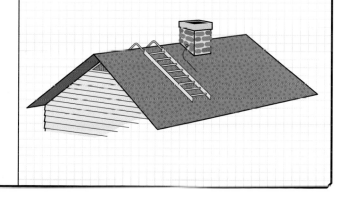

Chapter 4

ELECTRICAL SNAFUS

Electrical problems come fully equipped with more than their fair share of stress—and with good reason. We all know what electricity on the loose is capable of, so utmost caution should be used whenever approaching a repair situation that involves electrical current. But that doesn't mean that every electrical crisis needs to be left to the pros—especially at the hefty hourly rate a licensed electrician charges. Many small electrical problems can be easily handled by the homeowner equipped with a modest number of specialized tools and a modicum of sense.

> ## GO WITH THE PRO:
> ### The No-Shock Zone
>
> Working with electrical problems calls for even more caution than you regularly exercise with home-improvement projects. It's a wise idea to shut the power off at the breaker or fuse box—don't assume that the power to the circuit on which you're working is off because a wall switch is off. Call your power company if:
>
> + The main cable to the electrical meter has been knocked down.
>
> + Your lights flicker every time there's a strong wind.
>
> Other conditions clearly indicate the need for a licensed electrician; such as:
>
> + Any situation in which you are unsure of the correct course of action.
>
> + A live sparking wire or fixture.
>
> + All the power to the house is off because the main circuit breaker keeps tripping.
>
> + An electrical condition persists side by side with a flooding or plumbing condition.
>
> + A light fixture in your house consistently burns too fast through bulbs.
>
> + An outlet sparks or smokes.

4:94 **CURRENT BUZZ:**

Dimmer switches can set the mood, unless they set the light fixture to buzzing.

THE QUICK FIX Dimmer switches turn the current off and on many times per second to trick the eye into seeing a dimmer light. The problem is, all this work can make the lightbulb filament cranky and noisy. Try using a heavy-duty bulb known as a rough-service type, or one designed for use in a garage door opener and other physically demanding locations. If that doesn't work, you'll need to change the dimmer to a more expensive model that alternates the current in a gentler fashion (or do without a dimmer altogether).

| 4:95 | CAREFUL CAPTURE: |

Your broomstick air-guitar accompaniment to *Freebird* got out of hand and now your favorite lamp has a broken lightbulb still screwed into the socket.

THE QUICK FIX   First, unplug the lamp! Now, because a lightbulb fractures in sharp, jagged edges, trying to carefully unscrew the broken bulb barehanded offers a great opportunity to test your blood-clotting ability. Instead, use a pair of needle-nose pliers to grip the bulb base and twist it gently out of the socket.

DISASTER PREVENTION
Electricity Rules

Do:

+ Test with a noncontact inductive voltage tester to make sure power really is off—even if you think you've thrown the breaker or removed the fuse.

+ Use tools with rubber or plastic grips.

Don't:

+ Replace a fuse with one rated at a higher amperage.

+ Stand on a wet surface when working on an electrical circuit.

+ Touch plumbing pipes when working on an electrical circuit.

LAMP CHATTER:

Your peaceful quiet evening at home is less so because a globe lampshade is vibrating loudly.

THE QUICK FIX Glass globes—whether in a ceiling fixture with a fan or used on a table lamp—have a tendency to "chatter" even with minimal vibration. Put a stop to the noise by cutting dime-size squares of rubber from a rubber glove, tire-patch kit, or other source. Position a rubber square between the mounting flange screws and where they contact the glass. This will deaden vibration and restore the peace.

97

Fluorescent Lights

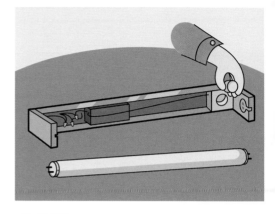

4:97   **STROBE SHOW:**

Your timeworn workshop fluorescent light is turning hobbies into headaches with its constant flickering.

THE QUICK FIX   Older fluorescent fixtures used a "starter" (modern versions are self-starting) to fire up the gas in the tubes. When the starter doesn't work, the light just flickers, never truly fully lit. In most fixtures, you need to remove the bulb to get at the starter, a round plug that sticks out through a hole in the housing. Check that the starter is seated properly in the housing and clicked into place. If it is, then it has become defective and needs to be replaced. Take the old starter to a hardware store or home center and buy a replacement with the same amp rating. Then plug it in and let there be (constant) light.

4:98 **STARTING GATE:**

The fluorescent fixture in your basement makes all the
right sounds but can't seem to get lit.

THE QUICK FIX

The key mechanism on any fluorescent light is the
ballast, a device that controls the current through
the light. The ballast is easily replaced by removing the faceplate
behind the light bulb and disconnecting the ballast body from the fixture's wires. Before replacing it, ensure the connections to the existing
ballast are secure. If they are, go ahead and replace the ballast. Word
to the dollar wise: it's usually cheaper to buy a whole new fixture
rather than replace the ballast in an older fluorescent fixture.

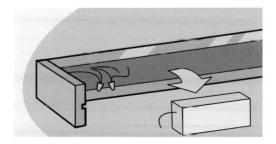

> ## ELECTRICAL TROUBLESHOOTING CHECKLIST:

Finding the real source of electrical trouble should be a process that starts at the most obvious solution and progresses from there. Before beginning any electrical repair, you should look at some of the most evident potential trouble spots.

1 > General power outage. Take the time to check lights and appliances throughout the house.

2 > Specific circuit tripped. Go to your fuse or breaker box to make sure the problem doesn't lie with blown fuse or tripped breaker.

3 > Tripped switch or outlet. Before jumping in to repair a light or other fixture, test the switch that controls it or the outlet into which it's plugged (to ensure that the breaker for that outlet is not tripped). Plug or screw a light you know is working into the outlet with the switch in the "On" position. Doesn't light? Most likely it's the switch. Check it with a continuity tester. This sounds like Greek to you? Call an electrician.

4 > The cord. Always inspect plugs and cords—some of the easiest fixes to make.

5 > Burned-out bulb. The simplest solutions are often the first to be overlooked.

4:99 NO RINGY-DINGY:

You're not getting your takeout food deliveries, because the doorbell isn't working.

THE QUICK FIX In most cases, this points to a bad doorbell button. Just unscrew the doorbell button, remove the wires on the back (low voltage, don't worry), and cross them. If the doorbell rings, it's indeed the button. Replace it with a similar unit from a hardware store or home center.

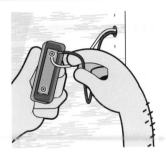

4:100 RELENTLESS RING:

A constantly ringing doorbell is a test of anyone's sanity.

THE QUICK FIX Because they see so much use, doorbell buttons (especially cheaper versions) are prone to shorting out with age. This is an easy problem to rectify. Unscrew the button housing and pull the button assembly out and inspect the wires. You'll find that they are touching at one point or another. You may have to check the wires as they run up into the wall. Once you've located the short, wrap electrical tape around it and reassemble the button.

4:101   **IN THE DARK:**

A wall or ceiling light won't work after you've replaced the bulb.

 THE QUICK FIX Cut power to the wall switch and remove it. Using the lowest setting on a multi meter's ohm scale, press one test lead to each of the switch's side terminal screws. With the switch in the Off position there should be no reading, but in the other there should be a complete electrical path indicated by a tiny resistance. Electricity should flow from the meter, through the switch, and back to

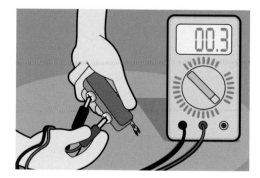

the meter. Replace the switch if it's bad. If it is okay, use needle-nose pliers to slightly bend up the brass tab at the bottom of the bulb socket. Reinstall the bulb and restore power to the circuit.

4:102   **CORDLESS SLUMP:**

Your cordless power tool just doesn't have the power that you know it should.

 THE QUICK FIX A cordless tool's battery is a likely culprit and you can measure its voltage with a multi meter. Run the tool until the battery has a small charge on it but is not completely discharged. Place it on the charger and when it is recharged, check it with the multi meter set to VDC (voltage, direct current). Use the next-highest setting above the battery's voltage. Press the test leads against the battery terminals (you don't have to match the test leads to specific terminals). A low voltage indicates that the battery is probably shot. Take the tool, battery, and charger to a service center.

4:103 | HELLO? HELLO?:

Your new cordless phone can't seem to hold a charge.

THE QUICK FIX Many times, this is simply a case of the base or cradle—through which the phone charges—being mounted or sitting at an odd angle. Clean the cradle contacts with pencil eraser, then swipe with a soft cloth and make sure the handset is sitting so that the "in use" or "charging" sign comes on.

4:104 | FILE FOR AN EXTENSION:

A device plugged into an extension cord isn't working.

THE QUICK FIX First, plug a known working device into the outlet and check the outlet's circuit breaker. Assuming the outlet is okay, take the same device and plug it into the cord. If the

>>>

device doesn't work, the cord is probably shot. Follow this with a multi meter test to be sure. With the multi meter set to its lowest ohm scale, press one test lead into one slot on the cord and the other test lead against the matching prong. A broken wire in the cord will produce a zero ohm reading, while electrical leakage between wires (that should be insulated from each other) will appear as an ohm reading if you test at the opposite prong.

> ### ELECTRICAL TESTING TOOLS
>
> The proper testing tools can make any electrical project a lot easier. Your tool kit should include
>
> + Basic volt-ohm meter (aka a multi meter). Serves as an all-in-one tester for checking resistance and voltage. New digital models are available from large home centers and tool outlets.
>
> + Neon test light. Can quickly tell you when a circuit or outlet is live.
>
> + Noncontact inductive voltage tester. Pen-shaped instrument that beeps and lights up as you move it close to an energized wire, outlet, or terminal screw—sounds exotic and expensive, but it's not. It's a lifesaver.
>
> + Continuity tester. Used to test if current can flow through a circuit.
>
> + Wire strippers. Essential when working with wiring; stripping with a utility knife or other tool can lead to accidents and a dangerous loss of wire.

4:105 | **TALE OF THE TAPE:**

You're trying to hang a power strip but just can't get the mounting screws in the right position.

THE QUICK FIX Electrical contractor Pat Porzio III offers this easy method: Apply a piece of tape to the strip's back and use a pencil to punch holes through the tape, centered in the hanging holes. Remove the tape and press it on the wall where you will hang the strip. Next, use screws to mark the wall through the holes in the tape. Drill on the marks and install the hollow wall fasteners for the hanger screws.

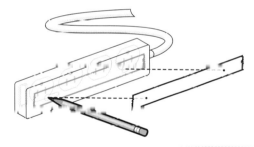

> **SAFE AND SOUND**
> **Plumb Shocking**
>
> Because the electrical system in modern homes is often grounded to the main water service pipe, you should avoid any contact with a home's plumbing when working on electrical connections.

4:106 | **RISKY FALLOUT:**

You try to plug a lamp into one of your outlets, but the plug just falls out.

THE QUICK FIX The problem might be with the prongs on the lamp's cord. If they are worn, severely bent, or seem loose, it's time to rewire or replace the lamp. If a new plug doesn't stay in the outlet, either, it's a simple but potentially dangerous problem. The contacts in the receptacle are worn and the receptacle needs to be replaced. Lucky for you, you can buy an inexpensive replacement receptacle at a hardware store or home center, and replacing it is merely a matter of turning off the power, removing the face plate, and switching the new unit for the old with the wires in the same places.

> **SAFE AND SOUND**
> **Extension-Cord Rules**

Different extension cords are intended for different uses, and using the wrong one can be to a fire hazard.

Do:

+ Use the shortest cord possible for the task.

+ Use only UL-listed cords (they carry the UL mark).

+ Choose a cord with a wattage rate suitable to the desired use.

+ Plug the cord into a grounded receptacle.

+ Use indoor cords indoors, and outdoor cords outdoors.

+ Unplug cords when not in use.

Don't:

+ Fasten down an extension cord with tape or fasteners.

+ Cover the cord with flammable materials such as a rug.

+ Connect one extension cord to another.

+ Use a long cord without uncoiling it.

+ Run cords through openings in walls, ceilings, or floors.

+ Drape cords over light fixtures or heating sources.

+ Use a cord that is very old, or showing signs of age, such as cracking.

+ Alter the plug blades on a cord.

4:107 | **HOT REPLACEMENT:**

You know you've blown a fuse, but you're not sure which one.

THE QUICK FIX Although, you can usually see a blackened mark or clearly broken fuse connection through the fuse window, sometimes it's not so apparent. If there isn't a fuse map (showing which fuse goes to which area of the house), you might be faced with trial-and-error to find the blown fuse. Instead, use a continuity tester: remove the fuse you think is blown, and press one side of the clip lead against the threads of the fuse and hold the test probe to the fuse tip. If the tester doesn't glow, the fuse has blown. If it does, move on to the next suspect.

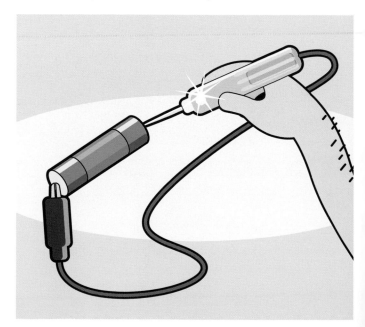

TRULY SHOCKING WEATHER:

A lightning storm is passing your way and it's got you worried about the health of your electronics.

THE QUICK FIX

Lightning can cause power surges even miles away from where it strikes. The wisest course of action to avoid damage to stereos, computers, microwaves, and other electronics is to unplug them during electrical storms. (A power surge can damage plugged-in appliances and components even if they are off.)

THE POWER-OUTAGE KIT

When the juice stops flowing, you need to be prepared to carry on until it can be restored. Here's a list of supplies that should go into any decent power-outage kit.

+ Candles and safety matches

+ Flashlight with fully charged batteries

+ Extra batteries

+ Battery operated clock

+ Battery-operated radio

+ Old-fashioned cord phone—sometimes called a "land line" (phone service still works in a power outage, but there will be no power for a cordless handset)

+ Pack it all in a cooler to be used for transferring chilled and frozen food if necessary

Chapter 5

PERPLEXING PLUMBING

The way water comes in and goes out of the home is one of those processes we take for granted—until we can't take a shower or make the toilet flush properly. A call to a licensed plumber can mean an expensive hourly fee, but the science of plumbing is fairly straightforward, and most problems are simpler to solve than you might think. So grab a mop and then turn the page—you might just be able to fix that dripping faucet on your own more quickly and with less effort than it takes to find a pro. And you'll avoid that big repair bill.

> ## GO WITH THE PRO:

Although most homeowners are surprised by how easy plumbing problems can be to fix, certain situations require greater expertise. For the most part, any major problem is best handled by a licensed plumber. These include

+ Where a water leak is severe and the collecting water threatens to cause damage to the home's structure before it can drain away.

+ Any situation in which raw sewage is backing up into the home.

+ In the event that the water supply to your home is entirely cut off and you don't know how to restore it.

+ When you can't find the source of a leak or the cause of a plumbing problem. When hiring a plumber, always check to make sure that he or she is licensed and has up-to-date insurance. Also be aware that your plumbing emergency may be covered by your homeowner's insurance—always check with your insurance carrier.

5:109 | ROYAL FLUSH:

You're spending a lot more time in the bathroom than you'd like because your toilet never seems to completely flush on the first try.

THE QUICK FIX   A poorly flushing standard toilet can be caused by a number of different problems. Lift the tank cover, and first check the chain that runs from the flapper cap to the flush handle; if it is too long, the handle won't lift the flapper cap sufficiently. Shorten the chain length by hooking into another link of the chain. Next, look at the water level in the tank—the amount of water affects how strong the flush will be. If the tank is not filling all the way (there should be a fill line on the inside of the tank), carefully bend the bulb of the float valve up a bit and see if the tank will fill. If it does not, check the toilet bowl rim holes (through which the water enters the bowl) with a small mirror, and if they are blocked, clean them with a small nail and acid-based porcelain cleaner. If none of the above does the trick, you may have a misadjusted or faulty fill valve that needs replacement.

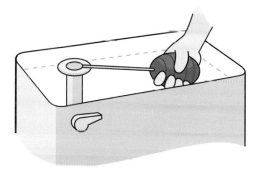

5:110 | **TANK GHOST:**

The phantom flush—that mysterious phenomenon in which your toilet seems to flush itself—can be little jarring late at night, not to mention a waste of water.

THE QUICK FIX The problem is usually caused by water slowly leaking from the cistern into the bowl because of a worn-out flapper valve. When the rubber flapper is compromised, it allows water to run out of the drain causing the toilet to constantly refill. Replacing it is easy—replacements are available at most hardware stores or home centers. Be sure to take the old one with you to find a correctly matching replacement.

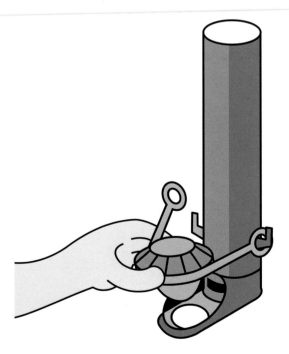

Low-flow toilets are a great way to save water, but sometimes yours simply doesn't flush strongly enough.

THE QUICK FIX   Ed Del Grande, an expert for the Kohler company and host of DIY Network's "Ed the Plumber," has dealt with many low-flow toilet issues. He says, "Always check the manufacturer's instructions to set the fill valve to make sure the water level in the tank is correct. For instance, most Kohler tanks have a proper fill line marked inside the tank. And a good rule of thumb, if there is no line, is to keep the water level a half inch below the top of the overflow tube inside the tank."

5:112 | **WATER WORKS:**

A constantly running toilet is testing your sanity.

THE QUICK FIX   The problem is most likely the flapper valve not sealing properly. First, make sure that nothing—such as a brick to raise the water level or a toilet-bowl cleaner dispenser—is blocking the valve from closing properly. This includes removing any mineral deposits around the seat beneath the valve. Also check that the pull chain attached to the valve is not too short and holding the valve slightly open.

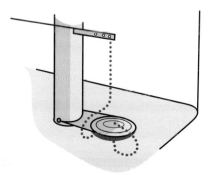

5:113 DRIP SERVICE:

A toilet tank is dripping, and you can't tell if the water is coming from harmless seasonal sweating or a bad seal.

THE QUICK FIX Dump some food coloring into the tank and see if the color reaches the floor. If it does, check the tank for cracks and the piping for loose connections.

5:114 RISING WATERS:

The toilet is about to overflow, and you know that your usual tactic of slamming the lid and crossing your fingers won't work.

THE QUICK FIX As soon as the level in the bowl starts rising, reach into the tank and prop up the fill valve (the ball or cylinder that floats on top of the water). That will stop the flow to the toilet, thwarting an overflow. The plunger, however, still awaits.

You've just stepped into the shower when some family member flushes the toilet downstairs and makes you a victim of shower shock.

THE QUICK FIX

In a busy household it's inevitable that someone is going to use the toilet when someone else is using the shower. The problem is that a toilet flushing draws cold water away from the shower, making for a quick and unpleasant temperature change. The answer is to slow the rate of the toilet flush so that the effect is minimized. Find the water valve to the toilet tank and close it until it is about a quarter to one-half turn from completely shut off. The tank will fill slower, but if it's the difference between second-degree burns and mild temperature fluctuation, that doesn't really matter, now does it?

> PIPE PROBLEMS

Leaks

5:116 | **STOPPER POPPER:**

The stopper-style plug in your bathtub isn't sealing the drain.

THE QUICK FIX — Unscrew the round overflow plate from the end of the tub and gently pull on the plate until the attached linkage assembly slips out from inside the tub cavity. The linkage is composed of several metal pieces, including a threaded rod. Turn the rod two or three revolutions to lengthen the entire assembly. Replace the linkage and screw the overflow plate and turn on the water. If water is still draining out, remove the overflow plate and lengthen the linkage a bit more.

5:117 | **STOP SWEAT:**

Sweating pipes are setting up a prime environment for mold in your basement.

THE QUICK FIX — Simple foam-pipe insulation is the answer to cold-water pipe condensation. Foam-pipe insulation can be cut to length and doesn't need to be used on every apparent pipe surface to be effective. Use it on pipes you can reach and you'll diminish the sweat on other lengths of pipe.

5:118 | **DRIP CONTROL:**

A pipe in your basement has made a puddle that is in danger of becoming a swimming pool.

THE QUICK FIX The first step is to turn off the water supply and drain the pipe if possible. Clean around the leak. Now cut a small length of garden hose, wrap it around the pipe, and bind it with two hose clamps tightened as securely as possible.

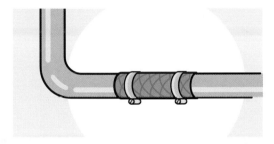

5:119 | **COLD HARD FACTS:**

The heat is off and you're seriously worried about your pipes bursting in the gathering chill.

THE QUICK FIX If it's too late to get to a hardware store and buy pipe-heating cable or wire, you can solve the problem with a heating pad. Move it to different areas of the pipe as they thaw and warm. As a fallback, you can also warm freezing pipes with a hair dryer.

5:120 **BAD VIBRATIONS:**

Your outdoor water faucet convulses into noisy vibrations when you turn it on, and stops only when the water flow is adjusted. How can you silence your faucet without stopping the flow?

THE QUICK FIX This is usually the result of a loose or defective washer. Once the washer is replaced, the sound goes away. To begin, shut off the water to the faucet by closing the globe or ball valve on the pipe leading to it. This valve is generally in the basement or crawlspace. If the vibration is coming from a bathroom or kitchen sink, turn off the water by closing the valve below the sink or closing the main valve supplying water to the house. With an exterior faucet, you remove the large nut immediately below the handle (the packing nut) to gain access to the faucet's interior. The washer is at the end of the faucet's valve stem and is held in place by a small roundhead brass screw in its center. If the screw is corroded, remove it and replace it also.

5:121 **PRESSURE PERCUSSION:**

Your pipes bang whenever you flush a toilet or abruptly let off pressure on a garden hose nozzle.

THE QUICK FIX The problem is most likely high water pressure. In addition to causing banging in your pipes (a condition called water hammer), high water pressure can erode washers and result in leaks. It also creates premature wear on appliances, including your dishwasher and clothes washer. Luckily, the pressure regulator on an incoming waterline is adjustable and you should try adjusting it before resorting to more expensive remedies, such as installing cushioning devices called water hammer arresters.

The typical inlet water pressure to a home is about 40 to 45 psi. Normally, it should not exceed 60 psi. The pressure regulator is usually preset to 50 psi. However, it can be adjusted anywhere from 25 to 75 psi with a simple turn of a screw, as shown here. To check the pressure, connect a pressure gauge to the nearest exterior faucet. These inexpensive gauges are sold at home centers in the same area as in-ground sprinkler components.

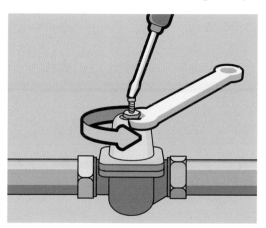

Pipe Movement

5:122 | LOOSE PIPES:

You're no plumber, but you know you've tightened those undersink pipes more than once and they still keep coming loose.

THE QUICK FIX Chances are, you've mixed PVC washers and nuts with metal parts (a common error when installing a garbage disposal). These connection parts must be of the same materials throughout the system.

121

5:123 | **NOISY HEAT:**

The knocking in the radiator is so loud that you're tempted to do without heat just to get some sleep.

THE QUICK FIX — Although knocking can be caused by a number of different things, the most common is air trapped in the line. Radiators have bleed valves (usually placed on the side of the radiator opposite from the inlet valve). Open the inlet valve (screw it counterclockwise) and then use a screwdriver to open the bleed valve, but be very, very careful because the water inside is probably going to be scalding hot. Bleed the radiator with a bucket under the valve until it runs a steady stream of water with no air bursts. As a rule of thumb, you should bleed all the radiators in the system at the same time. If that doesn't fix the knocking, you'll need to call a licensed plumber and have him check your boiler and heating system for other causes.

5:124 | **OUT OF TUNE:**

Every time you go for a glass of water,
you have to deal with a screeching faucet.

THE QUICK FIX It's a matter of rubber. Rubber washers age and harden and can make a particular sound when water passes over them in a hurry. If your faucet is making a screeching sound, it's most likely an older version with washers. Replace the washers with an inexpensive kit from a hardware store, or replace the whole faucet if it's time to update.

5:125 | **SOUND PLUMBING:**

A clanking faucet has you wondering if
your water supply is safe.

THE QUICK FIX A clanking, clicking, or mechanical sound signals a problem that needs to be investigated. Although it could be coming from the pipes, if it sounds distinctly like it is coming from the faucet itself, you'll need to take the faucet apart and reassemble, looking for cracks in any of the pieces and making sure that the entire assembly has been tightened well

123

5:126   SQUEAKY HANDLE:

The guest bathroom has a squeaky faucet that's starting to draw comments.

 THE QUICK FIX Sometimes the threads of the faucet stem become worn. The easy way to correct this is to remove the faucet handle and coat the threads of the handle stem with plumber's grease and then reassemble the faucet. This will usually make the handle easier to use and make the whole structure as quiet as it should be.

5:127   FREE FLOW:

Your friends are on their way over for a cocktail party, and the powder room faucet spits rather than streams.

 THE QUICK FIX The most likely culprit of an inconsistent water stream from a faucet is a clogged aerator—the screw-on screen that covers the mouth of the faucet. Remove the aerator and flush any lime or mineral deposits until the screen is clear, then reattach it. In cases where the aerator is entirely blocked or crusted, it's easier to just swap the aerator with an inexpensive replacement available from hardware stores and home centers.

FIX OR DITCH
The Lifespan of Faucet

Modern kitchen and bath faucets are generally well engineered and can easily last a decade or more depending on what type you have and factors such as how hard your water is. Many people choose to replace faucets as a design decision when remodeling, but there are more practical reasons that may lead you to replace a faucet. These include:

+ When its finish is worn away and its handle discolored or cracked.

+ The threads on the aerator or spout are worn or corroded, making aerator replacement difficult.

+ Its internal parts are so worn that replacement washers, O rings, screws, clips, and valve assembly simply don't solve the problem any longer.

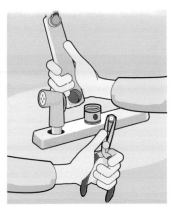

5:128   **SQUIRT ALERT:**

The kitchen sink sprayer offers a dribble where once there was a spray.

  Low flow in a kitchen sink sprayer is often associated with the diverter, a small valve located in the stem of the faucet. Take the handle assembly apart and pop >>>

out the diverter with a screwdriver and soak it in a bath of equal parts white vinegar and boiling hot water. Reassemble the faucet with the diverter in place, and the sprayer stream should be as strong as ever.

| 5:129 | SPOUTING OFF: |

You need to remove the tub spout, but taking it off seems close to impossible.

THE QUICK FIX Professional plumbers use a "strap wrench" to remove fittings that could be scratched, but chances are you don't have one of those in your toolbox. You can make do with a pair of slip-joint pliers. Jam the handles into the mouth of the spout until they are secure, and then turn the spout counterclockwise.

It will be days before you can replace the washer in your bathroom faucet, but by then you'll have severe sleep deprivation from the sound of the dripping.

 THE QUICK FIX Tie a long string around the end of the faucet so that the water drips onto the string and runs down it silently.

The water starts draining from your bathtub as soon as you have it filled.

THE QUICK FIX Many lever-action stoppers don't form a watertight seal against the drain. Fortunately, the fix is easy. First, unscrew the round overflow plate from the end of the tub. Gently pull on the plate until the attached linkage assembly slips out from behind the tub. The linkage is composed of several metal pieces, including a threaded rod. Turn the rod two or three revolutions to lengthen the entire linkage assembly. Replace the linkage and screw the overflow plate to the tub wall. Raise the control lever on the overflow plate and turn on the water. Check to see if the water remains in the tub. If it's still draining out, remove the overflow plate and lengthen the linkage a bit more.

5:132 | TOO HOT TO HANDLE:

Washing your hands can be a scalding experience. When it comes to tap water, how hot is too hot—and what can you do about it?

THE QUICK FIX Many water heaters have temperature settings well above 120 degrees F. Reducing the water heater's temperature is not only more energy efficient, it's also safer.

First, measure your hot water temperature. It's best to do this in the morning, before anyone has used any hot water. Turn on the tap and let it run for 2 minutes before reading the temperature with either an outdoor or a candy thermometer—just hold it under the water stream until the temperature is stable. If the temperature is 120 degrees F (or slightly above), you don't have to do anything. But if you're above 125 degrees F, you're in the danger zone (see chart). Here's how to turn it down.

The thermostat on a gas hot water heater is usually outside the tank at the bottom. On an electric water heater, look for two panels screwed to the top and bottom of the tank or one panel along the side of the tank—the thermostat will be located under these panels. The thermostat should be set on the "low" setting or within the "energy-efficient range." If the temperature at the tap is too hot at this setting, adjust the thermostat to a lower setting.

Wait 24 hours before testing the water temperature again (you might not get an accurate reading otherwise). Continue to test the water temperature and adjust the thermostat setting until the water temperature falls between 120 and 125 degrees F.

A Not-So-Slow Burn

This time-temperature burn chart from the Consumer Product Safety Commission illustrates how quickly a person can be scalded by excessively hot tap water.

WATER TEMP	TIME REQUIRED TO PRODUCE 1ST DEGREE BURNS	TIME REQUIRED TO PRODUCE 2ND DEGREE BURNS
116° F	35 minutes	45 minutes
122° F	1 minute	5 minutes.
131° F	5 seconds	25 seconds
140° F	2 seconds	5 seconds
149° F	1 second	2 seconds
154° F	instantaneous	1 second

Showerheads

5:133 | **WOBBLE CONTROL:**

Your gooseneck showerhead has broken free from the in-wall mountings, and its movement is likely to damage the tiles around it.

THE QUICK FIX First, pull the trim ring away from the wall. Next, inject foam sealant into the cavity around the pipe. This stuff expands, so apply it sparingly. Push the trim ring back in place and hold it for a minute or two to contain the foam sealant. The sealant will eventually harden, effectively locking the showerhead in position.

5:134 | **WEAKLY WASHING:**

Your morning shower feels like you're standing in a drizzling rain.

THE QUICK FIX The fine holes in a showerhead are easily clogged with mineral deposits and other gunk that is continually present in the shower. The first step is to try to clear the holes with the showerhead in place. Brush the holes with a stiff toothbrush saturated with a solution of equal parts white vinegar and lemon juice. Scrub hard and leave the solution on the showerhead for 15 minutes before running hot water at full force for 10 minutes. If this doesn't do the trick, you'll need to remove the showerhead and soak it in the solution, poking the holes clear with a thin paper clip or other tiny stiff probe.

129

> **K N O W   Y O U R   S T U F F :**
> **Caulk Talk**

Caulk. Wrong: A messy, gooey glop slathered into a gap. Right: A precision building material that is long-lasting and weathertight. Also known as: Sealant. "It all starts with making a proper choice," says Shree Nabar, DAP's vice president of technology, describing the need to choose caulk suited to the job.

WHERE	WHAT TO USE	TIPS
Bathroom	Siliconized acrylic "kitchen and bath" or "tub and tile." Also polymer types.	Check for disclaimer regarding whether caulk can be painted or time to wait before painting. Also check if biocide is added to fight mildew.
Concrete (where slabs meet or where they meet building)	Polyurethane or silicone.	Check disclaimer for suitability where abrasion is present. For sidewalks and slabs, look for produce labeled "self leveling." Crack repair using caulk is generally not durable.
Painting projects	Acrylic latex, siliconized acrylic.	Latex caulks clean up with soap and water.
Glass	Silicone and some siliconized acrylics specifically labeled for adhesion to glass.	Silicone is a durable caulk. Read the package disclaimer to determine if caulk causes corrosion to metal, making it inappropriate for sealing glass to metal.
Gutter	Butyl rubber types labeled as "gutter sealant" or "gutter and flashing."	These sealants are often available in a hand-squeeze tube.
Kitchen	Siliconized acrylic "kitchen and bath" or "tub and tile." And polymer types.	Check the package disclaimer regarding whether chalk can be painted or if you have to wait before painting.

WHERE	WHAT TO USE	TIPS
Roofing	Polymer types labeled for use with metal, masonry or asphalt roof products.	Many roofing sealants are available in two forms: gun grade and brush grade.
Siding, windows, doors	Polymer types, silicone/polymer, paintable silicone, butyl rubber.	Some advance sealants can be applied in wet or cold weather. Check disclaimer if okay for cedar siding.

Good caulking practice:

+ Apply in dry weather 50 to 90 degrees.

+ Use a foam backer rod on joints wider than 1/4 inch.

+ Always check disclaimer text.

I Works best when it adheres to two parallel sides.

+ Declines in performance when placed between perpendicular surfaces.

+ Poorest results when applied to three surfaces (two sides and bottom).

+ Tool to a concave shape.

Chapter 6

APPLIANCE FAILURES

Appliances are meant to

make our lives easier, which they usually do. Until, that is, they start leaking, heating imperfectly, burning toast they were supposed to brown, and generally malfunctioning. Although they may seem complicated, most home appliances work on fairly basic principles. And while there is a common sentiment these days that it's less expensive to simply buy a new appliance than to have it repaired, many of the minor problems that plague these devices can be dealt with using a minimum of time and effort. So the next time an appliance is on the fritz, consider the local landfill, and then decide whether to fix it or ditch it.

> **K N O W   Y O U R   S T U F F :**
> **Lubrication Basics**

Lubrication is often a two-step process. If the part is dirty, clean it with a solvent like mineral spirits. Next, lubricate the part per instructions in an owner's manual or using the guidelines on the chart below. For outdoor applications, remember to use a lubricant with corrosion inhibitor.

LUBE	WHAT IT IS	FOR BEST RESULTS
Bar-and-chain oil	Petroleum oil with antifling agent known as tackifier.	Use it in your chain saw. Wipe around the oil reservoir cap before removing it to keep dust and chips from getting in the reservoir.
Chain lubricant	Petroleum oil with corrosion inhibitors, tackifier and lubricity agents.	On outdoor equipment, use a lubricant formulated to be safe for O-rings. For heavy-duty indoor applications, use one containing molybdenum disulfide, aka "moly."
Household lubrication oil (spray or liquid)	Versatile petroleum oil for general-purpose lubrication.	Use it for indoor lubrication; door hinges, squeaky parts. Apply a tiny amount, work the part to spread it, wipe off excess. Outdoor-capable with corrosion-inhibiting agent.
Dry lubricant spray	A synthetic lubricant, like PTFE*, suspended in a solvent.	Use it where wet lubricant can make a mess or where lubricant film attracts dirt.
Graphite	Powdered graphite is a natural or synthetic form of carbon. The plate-shaped particles slide past each other.	Use it in locks and high-temperature industrial applications. Electrically conductive, it can accelerate galvanic corrosion between dissimilar metals in a saltwater climate.
Dielectric grease	Petroleum oil and nonelectrically conductive thickener/lubricant	A tiny dab on the side, not the bottom, of a bulb base, prevents sticking in the socket. A tube lasts years.

LUBE	WHAT IT IS	FOR BEST RESULTS
Paraffin wax	The residue from paraffin oil.	A handy, low-tech lubricant stick is a white, unscented votive candle. Rubbed on drawers, it makes parts slide easily.
SAE 5W-30, SAE 20W, SAE 10W	Light petroleum oils used for electric motors and pumps.	SAE 10, which is sometimes difficult to find, and SAE 5W-30 are often recommended for hot-water circulator pumps. SAE 20 is used for electric motors.
Penetrating oil	Light petroleum oil with corrosion inhibitors, solvents and additives that promote wicking action.	Use liquid penetrant on horizontal (faceup) applications, spray penetrant on vertical applications or horizontal (facedown) applications. Allow time for them to work.
Spray lubricant, PTFE additive	Petroleum oil with PTFE colloids and proprietary additives for corrosion protection.	For maximum lubrication, corrosion protection. Colloid particles improve lubrication by filling in tiny surface pits or by forming a separating film.
Spray lubricant with white lithium additive	Light petroleum oil with silicone colloids to improve lubrication.	A good-quality lubricant that performs well across a wide temperature range and offers good moisture resistance.
White lithium	Light petroleum oil with lithium.	Use it where thick lubricant film must cling and remain in place on horizontal or vertical surfaces.
Grease	Light petroleum oil or mineral oil*** with lithium, a clean-appearing lubricant and thickener.	Lubriplate Aero is excellent where low-temperature lubrication is needed. Solvent-free, it can be used in contact with most plastics without dissolving them.

*PTFE stands for polytetrafluoroethylene, a common high-performance lubricant additive. The best-known brand is Dupont Teflon. **Colloid particles so small they remain suspended indefinitely in a gaseous or liquid medium. ***A petroleum oil derivative that, in its highest grade, is a pharmaceutical-quality product with lithium, the lightest metal and a lubricant in its own right.

> **KNOW YOUR STUFF:**
> **How to Choose the Right Tape**

Tapes can range from ho-hum films with an adhesive layer to specialized products that leave glue (or even putty) after a backing is peeled away. There's an ideal tape for every job—but when in doubt, go for the heavier stuff.

TAPE	WHAT IT IS	WHAT IT'S FOR
Electrician's Putty	Synthetic rubber compounds, carbon black, granular filler on peel-off backing	Starts as tape, molds into putty. Forms around cable and pipe where they pass through siding, framing. Blocks water and bugs.
Glue Strip	Wax paper with adhesive bead.	Peel-off paper backing leaves 1/16-inch wide glue strip for light duty fastening, such as attaching small pieces of wood trim.
Duct	Fiber-reinforced plastic (7.7 to 12.6 mils thick) with rubber or synthetic rubber adhesive.	The thin, inexpensive type is ideal for strapping, bundling, patching tarp. The heavy-duty tape is appropriate for duct sealing. Both types damage a substrate when peeled away.
Electrical	Vinyl or PVC (7 to 8.5 mils thick) with adhesive that ranges from mildly to extremely sticky.	Small indoor electrical repairs can be made with the thinner variety. For outdoor use, buy the heavier, stretchable stuff.
Self-Fusing Rubber	Silicon rubber (20 to 30 mils thick) with peel-off backing.	Repairs and wraps hoses, electrical cable, tool and sport equipment handles. Flexible and stretchable.
Masking (General)	Crepe paper (4.5 to 5.5 mils thick) with rubber or acrylic adhesive.	Invented by 3M, it bundles materials and fastens paper. Note: Sunlight bakes tape onto surfaces, making removal difficult.
Masking (Painting and Heavy-Duty)	Crepe paper (5.7 to nearly 8 mils thick) with rubber adhesive.	Used indoors or out, heavy-duty varieties of this tape are suited for high temperatures and rough surfaces. Removal period ranges from seven to 14 days.

HIDDEN FASTENERS

Manufacturers like to make their creations as pretty as possible, which often means hiding the screws and clips that hold appliances together. This can make starting any repair a process of hide-and-seek. Places to look for hidden fasteners include:

+ Behind decorative faceplates or covers. Peel the covering back slightly and you may detect a small screw or fastener beneath, at corners or edges.

+ Under dials or slide controls.

+ Underneath simple plastic caps.

+ Plastic cases are sometimes held together with click-in tabs that are released by gently prying one face in from the other.

+ Metal covers with seams may conceal spring clips that are released by sliding a pry into the seam.

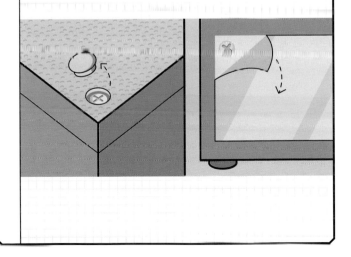

> HOME SYSTEM APPLIANCES

Air-conditioning

6:135   **DISCONCERTING LEAK:**

There's water pooling around your central air-conditioning unit (or perhaps dripping from the ceiling directly below the unit location).

THE QUICK FIX According to Glenn C. Hourahan, vice president of research and technology for Air Conditioning Contractors of America, it's likely that the drain pan for the air-conditioning evaporator coil is overflowing due to a blockage in the drain line. "Depending on the type of unit you have, the evaporator may drain to the outside of the house or to a floor drain in the basement. Either way, use a long wire (an unwound coat hanger will work) to clear any blockages that may occur near the mouth of the drainpipe. If that doesn't correct the problem, cautiously (you don't want to introduce much additional water into an already flooded pan) use a hose to force a short blast of water up into the drainpipe and through the drain trap and drain pan. This may free accumulated dirt and allow the evaporator to drain freely for some time." If that doesn't do the trick, Hourahan recommends turning off the air conditioner to avoid further water overspill and calling a licensed HVAC contractor to have a NATE-certified service technician address the situation.

GO WITH THE PRO
Signs of Central Air-conditioning Crisis

Central air-conditioning systems are fairly complex but, fortunately, fairly reliable. Beyond the simple power outage or clogged condensate drain line, more serious problems are best left to experienced, licensed technicians. Signs that should lead you to call for service include:

+ Unit running but no cool air coming out. If the appliance cools intermittently, it usually points to a problem with the refrigerant and may mean the system needs to be recharged.

+ Odd sounds coming from the condenser/compressor unit. Turn off the unit and call for service.

+ The system doesn't come on at all. First check the obvious culprits—that the thermostat is set to cool and that the appliance's circuit breaker is in the "On" position. Likewise, check all other system switches or disconnects. If these aren't the problem, make sure the air-conditioner is off and call for help.

+ Any significant leak or a dripping circuit breaker. This should be dealt with immediately by a professional. Turn off the unit and make the call.

Oil Burner

> **6:136** **HEATLESS IN SEATTLE:**
>
> The mercury is plummeting and you're trying to find all those extra sweaters because your oil furnace isn't coming on.

THE QUICK FIX Every oil-burner unit has a reset button that will trip from time to time. It's a red button on the box at the burner. Press it and the burner should fire right up, making your house a warm home again. However, do not try the reset button more than once.

> **GO WITH THE PRO**
> **Oil-Burner Meltdown**
>
> Some conditions are signs of bigger problems than most people can handle at home and require the help of a heating pro. According to John Levey, owner of Oilheat Associates in Long Island, New York, and the director of education for the Oil Heat Institute of Long Island, these include:
>
> + Chimney smoke. Oil burners typically give off smoke from the chimney and/or soot in the boiler room when combustion problems arise. These early warning signs indicate the need for professional attention and are often caused by minor problems that can be repaired quickly and inex-
>
> >>>

pensively. If they are not promptly repaired they can lead to more serious trouble and more expensive repairs.

+ Burner doesn't run. Oil burners require electricity to operate, so the first things to check are the large wall-mounted shutoff switch and the circuit breaker or fuse. If the switch and breaker are in the "On" position and the burner still doesn't fire, press the reset button on the primary control once. Never press the reset more than once because doing so can cause serious problems. If the burner starts and continues to run after the reset button is pushed it's important to understand that it went into reset for a reason. Chances are that there's a minor problem that requires professional attention.

+ Cycling too frequently. Burners normally cycle on and off numerous times during the day, but if the unit is continually cycling it may be a sign that the controls are not properly adjusted or, on warm-air systems, that the filters have become clogged. Before calling a professional, check your air filters and, depending on the model, replace or clean them if they've become clogged.

+ Odors. Oil heat systems should not emit odors. An odor can be a sign of an oil leak or of a combustion problem, both of which should be checked by a professional.

+ Safety Reminder: Call in the spring or late winter to schedule an oil-heat tune-up in late summer or early fall. Also there should be working smoke and carbon-monoxide detectors located throughout the house.

> LARGE KITCHEN APPLIANCES

Refrigerators

6:137 ARCTIC LIGHT:

Your frostless freezer is building an igloo from the inside out.

THE QUICK FIX
This can be the result of a leaking door gasket. The gasket allows the cold air to constantly seep out, making the refrigerator run overtime and produce extra chill in the freezer. Check the gasket by placing a high-power flashlight or emergency battery-powered light unit in the freezer with the beam pointed at the door. Turn the light off in the kitchen and check around the perimeter of the door. If there is any light leakage, you'll need to replace the gasket, which can be purchased directly from the manufacturer or from large-appliance retailers.

6:138 CHILLY DEPTHS:

There's a puddle of water under your refrigerator, and it's growing.

THE QUICK FIX
"I see this all the time," says Jeff McKinney, owner of JEM Plumbing and member of ServiceMagic.com. "Usually, it's because the icemaker line has sprung a leak. People don't realize that there's a shutoff valve. Typically, it's under the sink; if not, look in the basement, beneath the fridge."

6:139 **CHILL OUT:**

The party's in full swing, unfortunately your icemaker isn't.

THE QUICK FIX See if the icemaker actually got turned off by checking the wire alongside the icemaker assembly. If it's raised, the icemaker is off. Use the red lever to lower the wire, or lower the wire itself if there is no lever.

6:140 **INDOOR POOL:**

You've found a puddle in the refrigerator, but all the beers still have their caps on.

THE QUICK FIX The drain tube is blocked. Unplug the refrigerator and locate the drain plug near the back or bottom of the main compartment. Use a turkey baster to force a 50/50 solution of bleach and warm water into the tube. Repeat a couple of times, then remove and clean the drain pan located underneath the refrigerator.

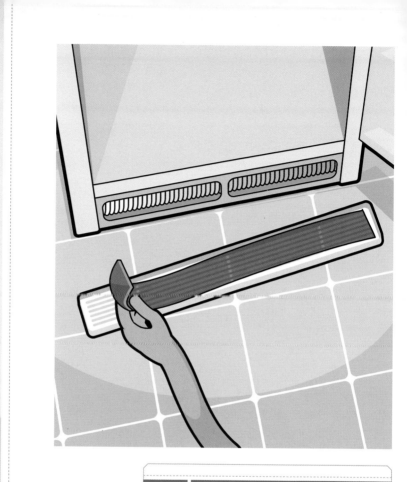

6:141 **THE HOT SIDE OF COOL:**

Your refrigerator is cycling on more frequently—and using more energy—than normal.

THE QUICK FIX The condenser coils underneath the refrigerator are a both a dispenser of heat and a magnet for dust—especially in homes with dirty kitchen floors or lots of pets. Clean the coils with a vacuum. You can keep further cleanings to a minimum by cutting a section of discarded pantyhose or a piece of lightweight filter material to fit inside the vent panel beneath the door, which should prevent most debris from reaching the coils.

> ## GO WITH THE PRO
> ## Refrigerator Warning Signs

The refrigerator is a fairly simple appliance and many small problems can be tackled by anyone with basic handyman skills. However, the presence of (in most cases, toxic) coolant under pressure and the sensitivity of the system itself mean that certain situations cry out for a more experienced hand. Call the repairman when

+ You hear a slight hissing noise and the refrigerator is not cooling as efficiently as it has been.

+ You feel an oily residue on the floor of the freezer compartment.

+ An accident results in the condenser coils being damaged.

+ The appliance is leaking significant amounts of water and you can't locate the source of the leak.

+ The outer shell of the refrigerator is sweating.

+ Unit continues to cycle on and off even after you have cleaned the condenser coils.

Dishwashers

6:142 | **DRIP CYCLE:**

The good news is that Fido doesn't have a problem, the bad news is that all the foam and water on the floor are from the dishwasher.

THE QUICK FIX　　When it's just water leaking from the dishwasher, you either have a misaligned door or bad door gasket. But if there is foam in the water, someone has loaded the dishwasher with liquid dish detergent under the mistaken notion that it is the same as dishwasher detergent. It isn't. Clean the soap dispenser and whatever residue you can out of the dishwasher, and dry the door gasket. Then run the dishwasher empty, without soap, for a couple of cycles.

6:143 | **STANDING WATER:**

The dishwasher won't drain.

THE QUICK FIX　　If you look inside the appliance, at the bottom of the swamp, you'll find what looks to be an upside-down cup. That's the "float" that controls the flow of water into—and more importantly, out of—the dishwasher. This can become stuck when it's

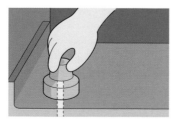

jammed with food debris or the errant piece of silverware. Clear the float so that it can move up and down freely. With free movement the float will activate the float switch properly. In turn, this activates the appliance's pump and the water will drain away.

6:144 DISH-GUSTING!:

Your dishwasher isn't living up to its advertised power—there are caked-on stains, your glassware doesn't sparkle, and you can't see yourself in your dishes.

THE QUICK FIX Although this could be a sign of a defective pump—requiring the services of a pro—more than likely it is a case of underheated water or clogged holes in the spray arm. Preheat the dishwasher water by running the kitchen sink hot water for a couple

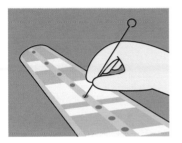

of minutes before starting the dishwasher. Periodically clear the spray arm holes by removing the lower rack to access the arms and gently cleaning the holes with a steel skewer or awl. (Don't use wood or plastic probes because they might break and clog the holes.)

Ranges and Ovens

6:145 RISE OR FALL?:

The temperature inside your oven is always a guessing game and every recipe you bake is at risk.

THE QUICK FIX First, check that the problem lies with the oven and not your cooking judgment: use an oven

>>>

⁂

thermometer to register if there's a variation between the actual temperature inside your oven and the alleged temperature on the control. If there is a difference, it is probably due to a thermostat problem. Check to see if the thermostat sensor tube has come loose from its mounting. Another cause could be that a portion of a rack or other metal piece, such as aluminum foil, is touching the sensor tube, which would create a variation in temperature. If these things check out okay, call in a pro or just rely on the oven thermometer, not the thermostat.

6:146 **WEAK FLAME:**

Your sauté is a mess because the pan is heating unevenly over the gas burner.

THE QUICK FIX Although they don't necessarily show it, gas burners inevitably become clogged with food particles and other kitchen grime, and the burner may provide a weaker flame on one side. If food is cooking unevenly in the pan, use a toothpick to poke all the burner-head holes clean, then turn the burner on a high flame and let it burn for 10 to 15 minutes to ensure all residue is burned off.

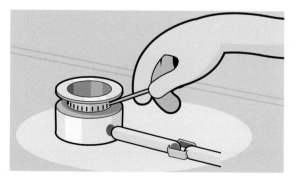

ALL CHOKED UP:

It's not emotion or allergies—the smoke from your stovetop isn't being handled by your range-hood fan.

THE QUICK FIX There are three types of hood systems, each of which can develop blockages. The first is a simple metal filter system that catches particles drawn up through the hood's vacuum fan. These should be soaked in hot soapy water mixed with a half cup of ammonia (avoid the fumes and handle according to the directions on the bottle). If the filter is very greasy, just replace it. Charcoal hood filters must be replaced if they are no longer filtering smoke out of the air. Some range hoods vent directly outside. If these are not evacuating smoke, look for a blockage at the vent, especially in the screening that covers the damper (including any exterior blockage, such as a growth of ivy).

---

5 GOLDEN RULES OF APPLIANCE REPAIR

1 > Be sure it's really broken before you fix it. Reset the circuit breaker, and make sure that the outlet the appliance is plugged into is live.

2 > Cut power at the service panel. Then unplug before servicing.

3 > Water and repair work don't mix. A wet floor is a slip hazard. Mop it dry before you work.

4 > Use a fluorescent worklight. These are cooler and safer than old-fashioned incandescent bulb lights.

5 > Safety glasses are a must. Dust, dirt, rust, and tiny parts can get you right in the eyes, especially when you're crouching in close.

Laundry Woes

You opened the dryer door to check your towels, and now the dryer won't start again.

THE QUICK FIX "Most dryers built in the last 10 to 15 years have a thermostatlike thermal fuse," according to Chris Zeisler, a former appliance technician and senior member of the RepairGuru staff at RepairClinic.com. "The heat-activated fuse prevents a fire in the event that the dryer severely overheats. Opening the dryer door in midcycle can trigger a heat spike that blows the fuse interrupting power to the dryer's motor circuit. Located on the heating element or gas burner housing or the blower housing, the fuse has a one-time life-span—you'll need to replace it when it blows. Replace the fuse and check the dryer ducting and venting that exits to the outside; poor airflow can be a contributing factor for the fuse blowing."

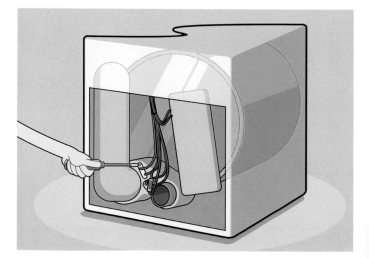

6:149 **TIME TO VENT:**

Your clothes dryer seems to have lost its zip—you need your favorite shirt and it's not getting dry.

 Clear the vent duct by removing the vent pipe and vacuuming out any accumulated debris from the pipe and duct. It's a three-minute fix that can save you a pricey visit from a technician.

6:150 **ON THE LEVEL:**

The washer is doing the shimmy 'n' shake even though you've been careful to level it and evenly distribute clothes in the basket.

THE QUICK FIX There's level, and then there's LEVEL. Taking a level reading off the top of the washer can be a problem, because it doesn't ensure that weight is being evenly distributed on all four corners of the washer. Make sure the adjustable legs are firmly in contact with the floor when leveling and that they are sharing the burden of the washer's weight.

> FIX OR DITCH?

With the fast pace of appliance innovations—new styles, new features, and new price tags—it's sometimes hard to make the judgment between fixing an older appliance and ditching it for a new unit. Although the decision is largely an economic one, it is also affected by intangibles such as how comfortable you are making repairs, and whether you want to upgrade as part of remodeling.

>> ELECTRIC DRYER

Ditch if ... gas is cheaper than electricity in your region. You might save on utilities by buying a new gas dryer, though you will incur the cost of adding a gas line. If you stay with an electric dryer, you still might save if you are replacing a truly ancient appliance that uses a timer instead of a moisture sensor to end the dry cycle.

But fix if ... you have to upgrade to meet requirements set by changes to the National Electrical Code. Electric dryers now use a four-prong plug and receptacle instead of a three-prong type. In some cases you might need to upgrade the circuit. That added cost may be reason to repair rather than replace.

>> WASHER

Ditch if ... you want to conserve. Today's front-loaders use less water (and less heated water) than top-loaders, and reduce drying time thanks to spin cycles of 800 to 1600 rpm (compared to 500 to 600 rpm for top-loaders).

If you do a lot of laundry, the savings can pay for the machine.

But fix if … you're concerned about the immediate impact on your budget of a new machine. Most washer repairs are straightforward. With a few basic fixes you could keep your machine chugging along for years to come.

>> ELECTRIC RANGE

Ditch if … Hard-pressed for time? New ranges with a convection option bake faster and more evenly while using a bit less energy than conventional ovens. Plus, if you switch from a difficult-to-clean, coil-top appliance to an easy-cleaning glass top, you might save enough time to use your new oven to do more than heat frozen pizza.

But fix if … it's purely an economic decision. An electric range has few complex parts, and the few it has are easily replaced. Ease of repair is reason enough to leave your range where it is. So is the need to upgrade the receptacle and wiring from three wires to four in many older homes. To have an electrician do this could increase the cost of the swap significantly.

>> DISHWASHER

Ditch if ... you are energy conscious. Newer dishwashers use less heated water and have more efficient pump motors, resulting in modest energy savings (slightly more if you choose an Energy Star appliance). Also a plus: quieter motors and more noise-dampening insulation.

But fix if ... the "total" cost is too great. Before you base your decision on appliance sticker price alone, look into installation costs. Plumbing and electrical hookups can tack on substantial costs, and that's if you can reuse the old water supply line. If not, you'll pay more.

>> STAND MIXER

Ditch if ... you are style conscious or a serious cook.
But fix if ... money is the issue. Most common problems can be repaired for less than half the expense of a new unit—if you can open a sealed gearbox and grease the gears, when you're done you'll be mixing again for a fraction of that.

>> VACUUM CLEANER

Ditch if ... the motor fails or if the unit is so old that replacement parts will be difficult to find.
But fix if ... it is a very expensive, very powerful high-end machine, or a lower-end machine that shows no sign of motor failure. Beater-bar belts are the first thing to go and are easy to replace. Clean out the vacuum head while you have it open.

>> WINDOW AIR CONDITIONER

Ditch if ... any significant problem occurs. Window air conditioners are on their way to becoming disposable appliances. Government-mandated seasonal energy efficiency ratios (SEER) standards rise every year, pushing energy use down, so a replacement pays its way from the moment you plug it in.

But fix if ... the problem is simply a reduction in cooling powers over several years of ownership—you probably just need a recharge of the coolant, which a reputable repair operation will do for far less than a new unit will cost you.

>> REFRIGERATOR

Ditch if ... the sealed refrigerant system goes. (Remember, take the doors off when you cart the bad boy to the curb to avoid child-entrapment dangers.)

But fix if ... the unit is experiencing minor but expected problems associated with aging, such as clogged drain tube, burned out lights, or a bad door gasket.

>> COUNTERTOP MICROWAVE OVEN

Ditch if ... you are not a microwave repairperson. Even a tiny microwave has a capacitor that stores several thousand volts as part of its power supply circuit. So you're probably better off tossing it or leaving it for the pros.

But fix if ... all it may need is a replacement of the $3 fuse.

>> TOASTER OVEN

Ditch if ... it won't toast. A broken toaster oven may be the most annoying trash bin candidate because a new heating element—if you can find it—will usually run the cost of a new unit.

But fix if ... it's been given a pet name and become a member of the family. Your call.

> SMALL APPLIANCES

Garbage Disposals

6:151 | **TRASHED SINK:**

The kitchen garbage disposal mechanism has frozen.

THE QUICK FIX "Ninety-five percent of garbage disposals have a reset button on the motor," says Chris Hall, a former appliance repairman and founder of RepairClinic.com. "No other appliance has this, so people assume they need to call a technician. I've answered literally dozens of calls that just needed someone to hit the reset." The button is small, usually red or black, and located on the bottom of the disposal unit under the sink.

6:152 | **FREE JAM:**

Your garbage disposal is busy humming but it won't do its job.

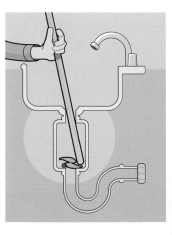

THE QUICK FIX Periodically, a disposal will jam and the blades need to be freed. Turn the disposal off at the fuse box and use a broomstick or the handle of a plunger to crank the blades free.

6:153 **SHARPER EDGE:**

It makes a lot of noise, but your garbage disposal just ain't cutting it.

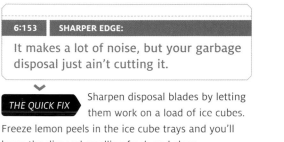

THE QUICK FIX Sharpen disposal blades by letting them work on a load of ice cubes. Freeze lemon peels in the ice cube trays and you'll leave the disposal smelling fresh and clean.

Small Helpers

6:154 **THE BIG WIND DOWN:**

That old electric clock may have a cool retro look, but it's noisy and slow.

THE QUICK FIX The gears in an electric clock can, over time, collect a lot of grime. An old repairman's trick is to turn the clock upside down for a couple of days. This allows debris and gunk to sift out of the gears and gets the clock back on schedule.

6:155 STUCK UP:

After a particularly wild blended-drinks party, your blender makes the sound but the blade doesn't move.

THE QUICK FIX When blending large amounts of liquid, especially if it's sticky, the blender blade assembly can become saturated with syrupy goo. According to Chris Peterson, author of *A Man's Whirled: Every Guy's Guide to Cooking with the Blender*, "Unless the blade assembly is cleaned right after blending, the

blade will be stuck tight with gunk that has collected in the housing. Simply soak the entire blade assembly in hot soapy water for about fifteen minutes, rinse thoroughly with hot water, and you're ready for the next round of frozen Margaritas."

6:156 IRON ORE:

You're getting steamed because your iron isn't, making ironing your shirts even more of a pain that it normally is.

THE QUICK FIX Mineral deposits from tap water can clog the steam pores in your iron, reducing the steam setting to a feeble drizzle. Fill the water reservoir with white vinegar, put the iron face down on a metal rack, such as the one you use for cooling cookies, and let it run on the "steam" setting until the reservoir is empty. The steam pores should be clean as a whistle.

6:157 **VAC ATTACK:**

You need to get the dog's hair up off the rug before the big Thanksgiving dinner, but even though the vacuum has suction, the bar won't spin.

THE QUICK FIX Your vacuum's belt is broken. In a pinch, you can make do for a quick cleaning with a nylon stocking stretched tight around the rollers and knotted securely.

6:158   WHAT'S THE BUZZ?:

The breeze from your standing fan makes the summer night bearable, but the buzz from its vibrating base is making sleep impossible.

 THE QUICK FIX Use felt furniture pads—available from home centers and hardware stores—on the legs of the fan. The felt will dampen the buzzing, letting you sleep sweetly.

6:159   WINDOW WATCH:

Your window air-conditioning unit is leaking.

 THE QUICK FIX You need to adjust the level of the unit. It should be slanted slightly to the back, to allow condensation to drain out of the back of the unit.

6:160 | **HEADS UP:**

The ceiling fan is making you nervous with its wobbly rotation.

THE QUICK FIX Generally, this is a sign that the fan blades are unbalanced. Duct tape lead weight strips, available from home centers, to each blade in turn and run the fan on low until you find the right combination of weight to stop the wobble. When the fan operates smoothly with no wobble, glue the weights to their positions.

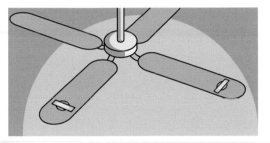

6:161 | **WARM RECEPTION:**

The window air conditioner is on high and you're still breaking a sweat.

THE QUICK FIX Always check that the fan intake control is on "closed" rather than "open." This is counterintuitive for most people, who think the fan needs to be open to circulate air. But, in fact, the open setting means that the air conditioner's fan is pulling outside—hot—air, rather than recirculating the cool air in the room.

Chapter 7

REFURBISHING FURNITURE

The furnishings in our homes

are subject to a great deal of stress and strain, from the weight of a thousand sittings, to casual spills made while watching the game. Upholstery becomes worn, legs get wobbly, and surfaces get dinged, dented, and scratched, all as part of the rough and tumble that is life in any home. We don't think of furniture as being dangerous, but a wobbly chair or an unstable bookcase is an accident waiting to happen. Good furniture is an investment, and even an inexpensive piece should serve you and your family for a number of years safely, and while maintaining a good appearance. Thankfully, most damage is reversible with very little expertise. You don't need to be a carpenter to produce long-lasting repairs that save money.

> **FIX OR DITCH?**
> **Furniture Longevity Guidelines**

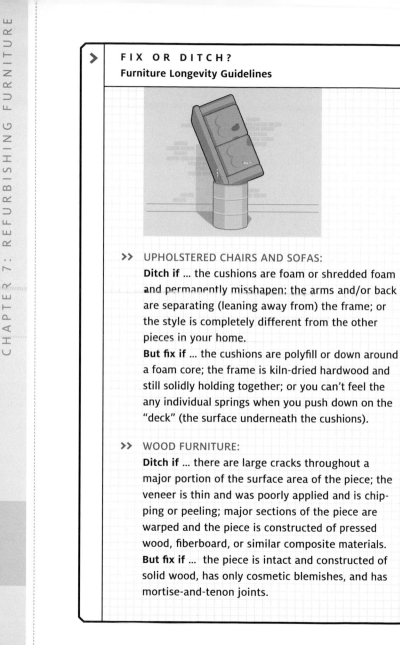

>> UPHOLSTERED CHAIRS AND SOFAS:

Ditch if ... the cushions are foam or shredded foam and permanently misshapen; the arms and/or back are separating (leaning away from) the frame; or the style is completely different from the other pieces in your home.

But fix if ... the cushions are polyfill or down around a foam core; the frame is kiln-dried hardwood and still solidly holding together; or you can't feel the any individual springs when you push down on the "deck" (the surface underneath the cushions).

>> WOOD FURNITURE:

Ditch if ... there are large cracks throughout a major portion of the surface area of the piece; the veneer is thin and was poorly applied and is chipping or peeling; major sections of the piece are warped and the piece is constructed of pressed wood, fiberboard, or similar composite materials.

But fix if ... the piece is intact and constructed of solid wood, has only cosmetic blemishes, and has mortise-and-tenon joints.

7:162 | **SLIP GRIP:**

Your leather sofa cushions keep slipping forward because of the slippery vinyl surface underneath.

THE QUICK FIX It's all a matter of friction, according to Leonard Lewin, author of *Shopping for Furniture: A Consumer's Guide.* "Position squares of rubber tool box drawer liner under the cushions to stop them from sliding."

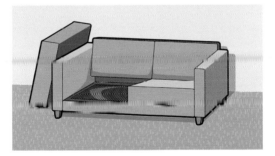

7:163 | **DIS-SUEDE DISASTER:**

Someone left a spot on your suede ottoman.

THE QUICK FIX Unless it's a soaked-in stain, spots on suede can be removed with an art gum eraser.

165

> IT'S A KEEPER

When disassembling or assembling furniture, avoid the frustration of a missing screw or other small part by keeping small, loose parts and fasteners in a closable sandwich bag. Then, even if you have to take time out in the middle of the project, you can keep all the parts from getting lost.

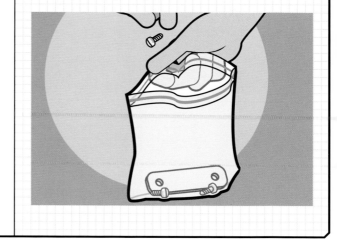

7:164   **HAIR TODAY:**

Your own personal Garfield the cat has left half his coat on your sofa.

THE QUICK FIX   The secret to a cat hair-free sofa (and any other upholstery, for that matter) lies in wiping the fabric with dryer sheets. The ionized sheets carry a charge that will have the cat hair jumping off the fabric and onto the sheet.

Your favorite overstuffed chair is two shades darker from dingy dirt, but you're not sure of the right way to clean it.

THE QUICK FIX Most upholstered pieces come with a code printed on their furniture tag: "W" means safe to clean with water, "S" means dry-clean only, and "X" means vacuum only. When in doubt, test-clean a small patch somewhere on the piece that is out of sight, or call in a professional cleaner.

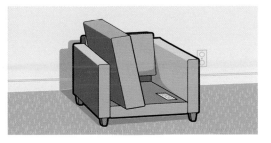

The kids had a bubblegum-blowing contest and your overstuffed chair lost.

THE QUICK FIX Mary Ellen, star of HGTV's *TIPical Mary Ellen* and author of *It Works! Over a Thousand New Uses for Common Household Items*, suggests, "Give gum the cold shoulder. Grab a frozen sports ice pack, a bag of frozen vegetables, or ice in a plastic bag and park it on the gum. Let the gum become good and frozen (replace the ice bag with a new one if need be) and, once it's hard through and through, merely chip it off the furniture."

Bedtime

7:167 | **SWEET—ODORLESS—SLEEP:**

The mattress smells as if the dog has found a new place to rest while he dries out after rolling on a wet lawn.

THE QUICK FIX You can deodorize and repel insects with one simple treatment. Make a mix of one part baking soda to one part crushed lavender flowers, and then dust the top of the unmade mattress. Let it sit for 30 minutes, vacuum off the dust, flip the mattress, and repeat on the other side.

7:168 | **COMFORT FLUFF:**

As the weather turns colder it becomes painfully apparent that your flattened comforter isn't doing its job.

THE QUICK FIX Comforters provide insulation and warmth by "loft," or the air spaces between feathers. Mary Ellen, star of HGTV's *TIPical Mary Ellen* and author of *It Works! Over a Thousand New Uses for Common Household Items*, says, "When feathers become compressed, the insulating quality of the comforter diminishes. To revive your comforter, toss it in the dryer with two or three new tennis balls and run the dryer on air-only setting (no heat)."

MATTRESS MAGIC:

The sag in your mattress has everyone rolling toward the center.

THE QUICK FIX Most mattresses need to be flipped regularly—once every two to three months—to stay in shape. You also need to rotate the mattress top to bottom (as well as the box spring, if you have one).

7:170 **THE PRINCESS AND THE PUNCTURE:**

An overnight guest spent a restless and uncomfortable night because you own a leaky air mattress.

THE QUICK FIX A bicycle tire repair kit can be used to fix the leak in no time.

> WOOD AND METAL FURNITURE

Working with Wood

7:171 | THE INVISIBLE PLUG:

You drilled without measuring, and now your bookcase has an extra hole.

THE QUICK FIX — Mix sawdust from the table wood with wood glue to create a thick paste. Fill the hole and scrape it flush. Then sand it completely level when dry.

DRIVING LESSON:

Making a small repair means driving tiny brads into your bookshelf, but you keep missing the nail and hitting wood or flesh and bone.

THE QUICK FIX Stabilize a small nail for driving by poking it through a piece of duct tape. The tape lets you hold the nail in place until you've driven it far enough in to be steady. Then remove the tape and finish driving the nail.

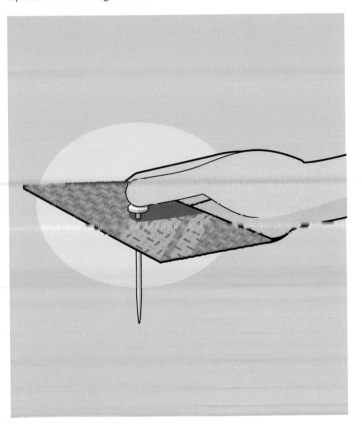

> ## KNOW YOUR STUFF:
> ### Abrasives

Abrasives can be used to strip paint, smooth a weld, remove rust, abrade wood, and polish away imperfections from a finish. Here's how to choose for the best results.

ABRASIVE	WHAT IT IS	WHAT IT'S FOR
Aluminum Oxide	A synthetic material derived from bauxite. The most widely used abrasive because of its toughness and versatility, it comes in the full range of grits from coarse pebblelike types to ultrafine sizes.	Suitable for smoothing wood, drywall, metal and metal welds, as well as removing paint and rust. Often treated with zinc stearate to make it less likely to clog with debris when stripping paint. Its most common application, wood sanding, progresses through 120-, 150-, 180-, and 220-grit sizes, which yield a furniture-grade surface.
Ceramic	An industrial-duty aluminum oxide. Available in medium, coarse, and extremely coarse grits.	A rugged abrasive best suited for heavy metal removal.
Emery	A natural material that combines aluminum oxide and a small amount of iron oxide. Commonly, a cloth-backed abrasive in medium and coarse grit.	Best for metal polishing because of its flexibility and the fact that it is not aggressively abrasive.
Garnet	A natural inexpensive abrasive. Typically used on lightweight papers in medium and fine grit.	Used for light-duty wood sanding, paint removal, and metal smoothing. Good for small hand-sanding jobs.
Silicon Carbide	A combination of synthetic and natural materials. Most often used on a waterproof paper so water can be used as a cutting lubricant. Almost always a fine to ultrafine abrasive.	Best at smoothing wood finishes, plastic, glass, ceramic, and nonferrous metal. The grits at the far end of its spectrum (1200 to 2000) are used for fine abrasive work.

>>>

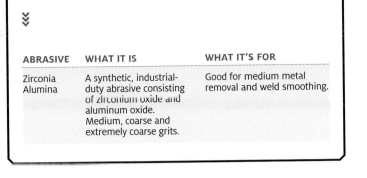

ABRASIVE	WHAT IT IS	WHAT IT'S FOR
Zirconia Alumina	A synthetic, industrial-duty abrasive consisting of zirconium oxide and aluminum oxide. Medium, coarse and extremely coarse grits.	Good for medium metal removal and weld smoothing.

7:173 HANDLING THE HANDLE:

The holes in your drawer knobs have stripped and the screws aren't keeping them in place.

THE QUICK FIX Push tooth-picks into the holes of the knobs and break them off, then tighten the screws. They'll grab the toothpick wood and hold tight.

7:174 SPLITTING UP:

You have to a drive a nail near the edge of a wood piece, but you're afraid of splitting it.

THE QUICK FIX Use the trick of professional carpenters: Before driving the nail, turn it over and hammer the point ⟫⟫

≫

a couple of times to blunt it. The flatter tip will crush wood fibers in its path, rather than prying them apart and leading to a split.

7:175   GUIDE GLIDE:

Your dresser-drawer guides are causing the drawers to stick.

THE QUICK FIX Simple drawer guides cause wood-on-wood contact and can, over time, lead to a lot of friction that creates a sticky situation. Give your drawer glide-power by rubbing a candle or bar of soap along the guides. Use a scented variety to add a nice aroma to the dresser.

7:176   HINGE SUCCESS:

You want the hinges on the kitchen cabinets to line up perfectly, but repeatedly removing and replacing the hinges is probably going to damage the brass screws, screw holes, or both.

THE QUICK FIX When fine-fitting cabinet-door hinges, use steel screws during the adjustment process until everything is right. Save the brass screws for final installation only.

7:177 | **TABLE TODDLE:**

Mealtimes feel precarious as your table wobbles and shifts.

THE QUICK FIX If a trip to the hardware store is out of the question, turn the table over, put a blob of silicone sealant on the bottom of the offending leg, and let it dry. Then flip the table over and it should be stable. However, you can do a more formal fix by purchasing nail-in leg guides (small plastic feet). Buy the adjustable kind to ensure you can stabilize the table. Use only one if a single leg is noticeably the short man out.

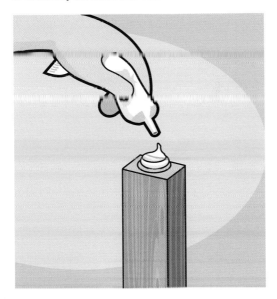

7:178 | **IT'S THE PITS:**

The baby's drumming has left a nice collection of craters on the surface of your pine kitchen table.

Small dents are a cinch to remove. Prick the surface of the dent several times with a fine-point needle and then cover with a moistened cloth. Put your iron on low heat and iron the cloth until it begins to steam. The moisture will infiltrate the wood and swell the wood fibers, filling out the dent. The steam will raise the grain so you'll need to lightly sand after raising the dent. Note: A word of caution! Don't use this technique on a table covered in veneer—the veneer will separate and peel up once you steam the underlying adhesive.

7:179 | **COVER YOUR TRACKS:**

How many times have you been asked to use a coaster? Now you have to find a way to get rid of those water rings on the wooden coffee table.

Drip a few drops of machine oil on the surface of the wood and mix in some ground pumice (available at home centers) to make a loose paste. Rub the paste around the rings with the tip of your finger until the rings are gone, then wipe off the paste with a damp cloth and dry the surface.

7:180 SPECIAL PLACES:

You notice that the finish is wearing on the dining table in the places where the family always sits.

THE QUICK FIX A common problem, says Leonard Lewin, author of *Shopping for Furniture: A Consumer's Guide.* His suggestion: "Rotate the dining room table just as you would a mattress. Small families tend to sit at the same places, causing undue wear at those points on the table. Rotating evens out the wear."

7:181 WAX AND WANE:

That candlelit dinner gave you a memorable evening, but the wax blobs on your wood table are making for a depressing day after.

THE QUICK FIX Don't despair. Freeze the wax with a freezer-pack or an ice cube in a plastic bag. When hard, the wax can be chipped off the table with the edge of a credit card.

Chair Challenges

7:182 | **RUBBER MEETS THE ROAD:**

The metal legs of your kitchen chairs cut right through their end caps, scratching your linoleum.

 THE QUICK FIX
Replace the end caps with new rubber leg tips (available at home centers) and stuff a coin or metal slug inside each tip before slipping it on the end of the chair leg. The coin or slug prevents the end of the leg from cutting into the rubber tip.

7:183 | **RUNG OUT:**

One of your dining room chairs is complaining and splaying every time someone sits down on it—a lawsuit could be only a matter of time.

 THE QUICK FIX
Over time and prolonged use, chair rungs can work themselves loose. The simplest way to remedy the situation is to inject white woodworker's glue around the rung and clamp the legs until the joint dries. Chances are, you don't have woodworking clamps lying around, but don't let that stop you. Strap a belt around the legs, compressing them together by notching the belt as tightly as

possible. Once the glue dries, chisel any excess glue that has bled out, and the chair will be stable once again.

7:184 **ROCK ON:**

That favorite rocking chair is in danger of leaving its mark on your lovely—not to mention expensive—hardwood floors.

THE QUICK FIX Line the bottom of the rocking-chair runners with the self-adhesive protective felt stripping often used on the bottom of doors. You can find it at hardware stores and home centers.

> ### KNOW YOUR STUFF:
> **Adhesives**

With these six adhesives, you can make—or fix—just about anything.

ADHESIVE	WHAT IT IS	WHAT IT'S FOR
Construction Adhesive	A blend of elastomers* and resins with water or solvent (or a polyurethane blend with limestone). It's usually extruded out of a tube, though trowel-grade types, which have a longer open or working time, are available.	Specific—usually big—jobs and materials, such as fastening plywood to floor joists or paneling to drywall. Clamping pressure (also called fixturing) is supplied by the weight of the workplace or by driving a fastener through the joint between the pieces.
Epoxy	A two-part adhesive consisting of a resin and a curing agent. Its consistency can range from a liquid, to a gel, to a putty stick that is kneaded to mix the inner and outer layers (resin and curing agent).	Unusual bonding and repair jobs when the joint does not fit tightly or when a portion of the repaired area needs to be rebuilt with the epoxy itself. Also good for filling holes and cracks. Epoxies have excellent heat resistance and high strength, but can be brittle in cold temperatures. Some cure under water or on wet surfaces. No clamping pressure or only light pressure is required.
Cyanoacrylate	A single-component adhesive that cures extremely quickly in the absence of air and requires a small amount of moisture in the material to be fastened. Sometimes referred to as "super glue."	Making a rapid bond when the glued parts are brought together with just hand pressure. Good for bonding porcelain, glass, and some rigid plastics.

ADHESIVE	WHAT IT IS	WHAT IT'S FOR
Polyurethane Glue	Urethane polymer and catalyst blend that requires moisture to cure. The moisture can come from the surfaces being bonded or the air.	Joining wood to wood when a water-proof joint is required. However, it can be used to join almost all common building materials. Urethane wood glues expand as they cure, foaming slightly in the process. To keep the joint stable during curing, it requires evenly distributed clamping pressure. Urethane construction adhesives do not foam, but cure much more slowly than comparable products.
White Glue	A syruplike emulsion consisting of polyvinyl acetate resin suspended in water.	General household adhesive bonding involving wood, paper and fabric. It's especially good at bonding wood to wood. For maximum strength, the glued joint requires clamping pressure. This produces an extremely thin joint line that's difficult to detect. Does not produce a moisture-resistant assembly.
Yellow Glue	A thick emulsion of polyvinyl acetate or aliphatic resin suspended in water (plus additives that increase its stickiness and reduce its dry time).	Often used with clamps to produce a thin, almost undetectable joint line when gluing wood. Also excellent for general household adhesive bonding. Has increased moisture resistance compared to white glue. Can be used without clamps when fastening small pieces of wood in finish carpentry.

*Elastomer: a substance capable of returning to its original size after being stretched.

Storage

> **SAFE AND SOUND**
> **Stop the Tumble**
>
> Tall bookshelves can easily become top-heavy without your noticing it; and a fully weighted bookshelf that falls over can cause serious injury—not to mention considerable damage—to the shelves and items stored on them. Secure tall bookshelves to the wall with an eyehook strap (manufacturers often include them with the bookshelf, or you can buy them at large home centers).

7:185 **SPINAL TAP:**

All those ponderous books you love are causing your bookshelves to sag.

THE QUICK FIX Installing a central wood support piece will reinforce the shelf, but detract from the look of the bookcase. Disguise it by buying an inexpensive used book that is as thick as, and slightly taller than, the support piece. Cut off the spine of the book and cut it to size, then laminate it to the wood support using white carpenter's glue.

7:186	AIR APPARENT:

Aunt Ethel left you that incredible antique wardrobe...complete with an ancient smell.

THE QUICK FIX — Put crumpled brown-paper bags in the closed wardrobe for a few days. Discard the bags and air the wardrobe—weather permitting, preferably outside in the sunshine—for a week or more. It's not exactly quick, but it will fix the problem.

7:187	PEELING CABINETRY:

The laminate has come off the corners of your kitchen cabinet doors and you don't want to buy new ones.

THE QUICK FIX — Have a careful look at the corner of the door where the laminate is peeling up. If the core of the door appears to be sound, then the repair is simple. Use a fine-tooth hacksaw blade or a putty knife to spread some moisture-resistant adhesive under the laminate. Then use masking tape wrapped from the front of the door and around the edge to pull the laminate down. Remove the tape once the adhesive has set, and use a razor-sharp chisel to pare off globs of adhesive that squeeze out from under the laminate while they are still soft. This should yield good results. However, if moisture from cooking or cleaning has caused the core of the doors to crumble or otherwise fail, you're better off replacing those doors, or replacing all the doors in the kitchen. You will find it very difficult to make the laminate adhere properly to a deteriorated substrate.

Chapter 8

YARD AND GARDEN DILEMMAS

The elements play havoc

with any exterior part of your home, from a garage door to a walkway—and then there's the fact that yards and gardens tend to attract more than their fair share of visitors with destructive tendencies. Damage to the outside of your home isn't just a cosmetic concern that detracts from its curb appeal— you want to prevent whatever is harming the exterior from invading the interior. Being exposed means your property and outbuildings suffer more, and more varied, problems than any other part of your house. Fortunately, there are also more quick fixes available for the great outdoors.

> ### GO WITH THE PRO
> **Barrier Concerns**
>
> Although small stains and cracks can usually be
> fixed with store-bought products and a little elbow
> grease, bigger troubles in your home's masonry
> walls call for more expertise. Bring in a mason or
> structural professional when:
>
> + A crack in a masonry wall is large and
>   growing rapidly.
>
> + A foundation wall appears to have shifted.
>
> + You find large patches of black mold on the wall.
>
> + The wall is actually buckling
>
> + Bricks, mortar, or stucco simply crumble away to
>   dust at your touch.

Pest Patrol

8:188 | **INVADING ARMY:**

Ants are moving in from outside, and
you don't want to use a toxic brew to
defeat them.

THE QUICK FIX — "A 50/50 mix of peppermint oil
and water will get rid of ants," says
Amy Devers, cohost of the DIY Network's *DIY to the
Rescue* show. "Fill a spray bottle, and spray wherever
you see them coming out of hiding."

8:189 **ON A ROLL:**

The power to your garage is out with the door shut, and you need to get your car out or you'll have to take a bus.

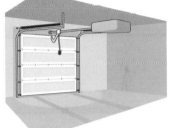

THE QUICK FIX You'll notice a cord—usually with a red handle—dangling down from the guide track that the opener uses to open and close the door. This is the manual override. Once pulled, it allows you to open and close the door with your own power in the form a little elbow grease.

8:190 **FROZEN OUT:**

Cold weather has stiffened the mechanism of your garage door opener and caused it to lose power.

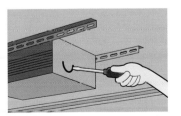

THE QUICK FIX Most garage door openers made in the past 15 years have pressure adjustments for both raising and lowering. Check and adjust these settings seasonally to keep things running smoothly.

That sagging garage door is getting harder and harder to open.

THE QUICK FIX Garage doors, especially older, wooden models, are as susceptible to the ravages of time and gravity as the rest of us. If your aging doors are a little saggy, square them up with the tension rods positioned on the back of the door. The rods are placed diagonally from top to bottom corners and can be tightened at a turnbuckle to straighten out the door—do a little at time to allow the door to adjust to the change. If your door isn't already equipped with tension rods, you can buy them at home centers.

8:192 | DOOR LINES:

Your dream car is parked in out of the elements, but it's not secure because the garage door won't lock.

THE QUICK FIX Most garage doors have two horizontal bars that move out from the center of the door into slots along the side of the door in the door track, effectively locking the door in place. Over time, these bars can shift slightly out of position so that they are no longer correctly aligned with the locking slots. To realign the bars, unscrew the guide brackets on the edges of the door so that they are loose enough to move, and then reposition them so that they smoothly guide the locking bars into the locking slots. Lubricate the lock mechanism with machine oil and you're done.

8:193 **BLACK BLOT:**

After working on the car, you find a big oil stain on the driveway.

∨

THE QUICK FIX Pulverize a scrap piece of drywall with a hammer (any new home construction site will have dumpsters full of waste pieces of drywall). Crumble the pulverized drywall with your hands and sprinkle on the stain. Leave it overnight, and rinse off in the morning. Reapply and brush in with a bristle broom in cases of stubborn stains.

> YARD TRIALS

Patios and Decks

| 8:194 | BOULDER EVICTION: |

Clearing the way for your new backyard deck, you've encountered the proverbial immovable object.

THE QUICK FIX The task is to get the boulder up out of its resting place so that you can roll it out of the way. The secret to doing this is—as your high school physics teacher taught you—leverage, dear homeowner, leverage. Dig a small hole down under one side of the boulder, stick a lever in the form of a two-by-four under the rock, and set a fulcrum (a small chunk of waste wood will do) under the two-by-four. Do the same on the opposite side of the rock. Work each side a little at a time, slipping increasingly larger amounts of earth, pieces of wood, or stones underneath the boulder until you can simply roll it out of its resting place onto flat ground. From there it should be a relatively simple chore to roll it where you want it.

CITRUS SOLUTION:

A big orange rust stain makes your concrete patio a major summer eyesore.

THE QUICK FIX Rub a lemon or lemons over the stain until it is saturated with lemon juice, then put a piece of plastic over the stain. Leave it for two to three hours, and then hose off. The stain should be gone. If some stain remains, repeat the process.

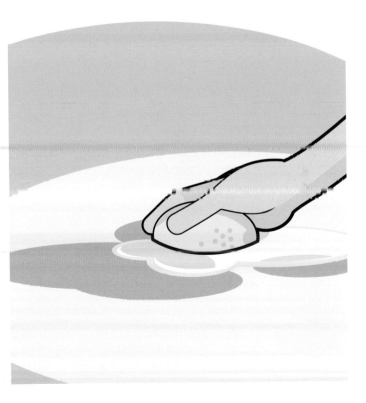

8:196 ALL DECKED OUT:

That precious deck you installed last summer is getting stained by the moisture collecting under your container plants.

THE QUICK FIX Cork drink coasters are attractive and simple ways to get the base of plant pots or the saucers underneath up off the surface of the deck. Use a triangle of three stacks of two coasters each under the container and the airflow will keep everything dry and the wood stain-free.

8:197 SLIP RESISTANCE:

Every time it rains, your deck stairs become hazardously slippery.

THE QUICK FIX Provide traction on aging wood stairs by nailing or gluing down strips of asphalt roofing shingles, or strips of outdoor carpeting.

PATIO PEEVE:

A single cracked paver is ruining the look of that patio you so meticulously laid.

THE QUICK FIX

Any paver set in a bed of sand can be removed without tearing up big sections of the surface. Simply bend the bottom two inches of two barbecue skewers at 90-degree angles, using a vise and pliers, then slip the bent ends down alongside either side of the paver, turn, lift the cracked paver right out and replace with a new one.

8:199   **SHADY DOINGS:**

Your deck is becoming smelly and slick, thanks to a growing patch of mildew.

THE QUICK FIX

Scrub the deck with a solution of one cup bleach to one gallon warm water and rinse with cold water immediately after. To discourage mildew from coming back, cut back any overhanging trees that shade the deck, and make sure that container plants and other moisture sources are not keeping the deck wet for long periods.

Fences and Walkways

> **8:200** **ASKEW GARDENS:**
>
> The garden looks a bit snaggle-toothed with your wobbly fence posts adding weird angles to the landscape.

THE QUICK FIX Fence posts can come loose when the ground around them shifts, or when they begin to rot. Either way, the fastest, easiest solution is a "sister" post. You'll need lengths of two-by-four that have been treated with preservative. Dig down about six inches below the bottom of the post on the two sides to which it leans. Position the two-by-fours so that they run from the bottom of the new hole up to the first rail of the fence, and screw them in place to the original post. Fill in the hole and compact the soil—the fence will be as sturdy as if it were new.

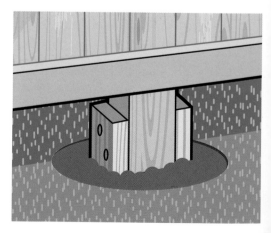

You've got the house and the white picket fence, but a drooping gate is ruining the dream.

THE QUICK FIX   Wear and tear and the elements combine to make picket-fence gates droop, but handymen have long used an easy fix straight from geometry class. Install an eye screw in the frame of the gate, about where it connects to the upper hinge. Attach a strong cable to the eye screw using a clip available at home centers, and fasten another cable kitty corner to the first, at the bottom outside of the gate frame. Now join the two cables with a turnbuckle, tightening until the gate is back in square.

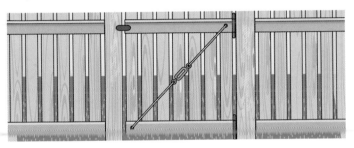

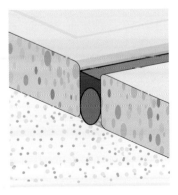

The joints in your concrete walkway have deteriorated, making a simple stroll into an obstacle course.

THE QUICK FIX   Sidewalks and other concrete paths are laid with "expansion joints"—gaps between sections

>>>

that are filled with wood or special fiberboard—to accommodate expansion and contraction of the concrete. Unfortunately, over time, the joint material can weather away. Remove it with a cold chisel or utility knife, clean the joint well, and stuff foam backer rod (available from home centers) into the crack, using a putty knife. Seal the joint with an exterior caulk or other sealant designed to be used with masonry, and everything will be on the level once again.

8:203	DON'T TOIL, BOIL:

You'll go mad trying to keep the weeds out of the cracks between your sidewalk slabs.

THE QUICK FIX Kill weeds fast by pouring boiling water directly on them. "Put a kettle of water on the stove or simply reuse the water you've just boiled pasta in," says Amy Stewart, author of *The Earth Moved: On the Remarkable Achievements of Earthworms*.

"You can add salt or plain vinegar to the water for extra power, but make sure the mixture doesn't come into contact with your lawn or any plants you don't want to kill." Plan on repeating the treatment about once a month if weeds resprout.

Protecting Plants

8:204 **FENDING FELINES:**

The neighborhood cats treat your garden
beds as one large litter box.

THE QUICK FIX Cats like their own smells to be the strongest ones
wherever they're making their mark, so you need to
ward them off with strong smells. Chili powder or crushed-up moth balls
sprinkled around the beds will usually solve the problem.

8:205 **PET PEEVE:**

The neighbor's
Rottweiler has been
digging craters in your
rose bed, but you're
not man enough to
face him down.

THE QUICK FIX You can take
two approaches
or combine them for best effect.
For the times when you're just sitting around enjoying the view, set
up sprinklers in areas where the

>>>

dog normally digs. When he arrives and begins excavating, hit the sprinklers and, after a few times, he'll get the message. If you're not a fan of sitting around waiting for a dog to show up in your garden, dig down in the dog's favorite areas and put down a layer of chicken fencing about an inch below the surface of the dirt. Dogs hate scraping their paws on the stuff and will leave the yard alone after they encounter it a couple of times.

| 8:206 | **BULB BARRIER:** |

Burrowing varmints are eating through your crop of tulips before they bloom.

THE QUICK FIX Rather than bury bulbs individually, dig out a "tray" bed, line it with chicken wire or other metal mesh, and put the bulbs on top. Burrowers will not be able to penetrate the barrier and your flowers will come up as planned.

| 8:207 | **BUG BLAST:** |

Houseplant pests are a part of the great outdoors that you just wish would stay there.

THE QUICK FIX Take a trip to the kitchen. According to Andrew Lopez, author of *Natural Pest Control, Alternatives for the Home and Garden*, "A few small cloves of garlic shoved just below the surface of the soil in your houseplants will send most bugs packing. You can also make a tea from it and spray the plants."

8:208   **TOP HEAVY:**

Every stiff wind sends your tall container plant head over heels.

THE QUICK FIX   Taller plants can easily become top heavy, with a tendency to fall over at the slightest provocation. Keep them in the upright position by placing the plant's pot in a larger decorative pot, filling the space between the inside and outside pots with sand or decorative pebbles.

8:209 | **OVER-WEIGHTY:**

Moving your container plant is cause for a call to the chiropractor.

THE QUICK FIX Large garden pots filled with soil (and water) can become extremely heavy, stressing deck structures as well as your back. When planting containers, fill in the bottom quarter of the pot with shredded plastic bottles, cut-up egg cartons, or Styrofoam packing material. The lightweight materials take up space and create air pockets that help increase drainage, while at the same time making the pot a whole lot easier to lift.

8:210 | **WILT NOT:**

Those cut flowers you brought home yesterday look past their prime already.

THE QUICK FIX A few simple steps keep cut flowers looking good and increase their staying power: Always recut stems under running (warm) water, and immediately place in lukewarm water in a vase. Add a couple drops of bleach to prevent fungus, and half a teaspoon of sugar to the vase water and your cut flowers might even forget they've been cut. For maximum shelf life, change the water everyday.

WATER WORKS:

Every time you water your houseplants, you start a delayed-reaction Niagara Falls.

⌄

THE QUICK FIX   Small houseplant containers and the light sterile soil combine to ensure that water runs right through, even in small amounts. The answer is to stick a few ice cubes into the soil each morning. Water will drip slowly down as the cubes thaw and be absorbed by the roots before any extra overflows.

Gardens

8:212   **ROCK AND ROLL:**

Trying to make a lovely rock garden on that slope in your backyard you suddenly discover you can't lift a 110-pound rock!

⌄

THE QUICK FIX   Keep on trucking. Hand trucks are not only an essential moving tool they can be indispensable around the garden. Use the hand truck to move the rocks exactly where you want them, then just slide the nose out from underneath the rock and you're done.

8:213 **A FINE EDGE:**

You're not ready to start digging because you're having a hard time envisioning what shape your new flowerbed should be.

THE QUICK FIX   Lay out and adjust the shape of a flowerbed quickly and easily with the help of a garden hose. Position the hose in the shape you want, and change it until it looks right. Then use it as a guide to dig out the edges of the bed.

8:214 **SPEAR FACTOR:**

A weed-ridden asparagus patch has you about ready to give up on your favorite crop.

THE QUICK FIX   Add salt. "Asparagus is the only vegetable that can withstand salt," says Penny Griggs, an organic farmer in Vermont. "Spreading salt around your plants will kill the weeds but leave your asparagus unharmed."

8:215 **SUN-DRIED TOMATOES:**

You need a way to water sensitive tomato plants during your summer vacation, without asking your neighbor to take care of them (again).

THE QUICK FIX Collect some liter-size plastic soda bottles and punch a few small holes in each one. Then, bury a bottle up to its neck next to each of the plants. Before you leave, simply fill the bottles; they'll slowly release the water over the next four or five days and keep your plants from wilting.

8:216 **NOT EASY BEING GREEN:**

Even though you regularly mow, your browning lawn is buying you dirty looks from your neighbors.

THE QUICK FIX If you remove more than one-third of the height of the grass when mowing, it can stress the grass, which leads to—you guessed it—browning. Adjust the height of your mower to a higher setting and mow more frequently. You'll have happier, greener grass.

> OUTDOOR RECREATION //////////////////////

Pool Maintenance

> ### GO WITH THE PRO
> **Watery Woes**
>
> Pool systems are not overly complicated, but certain
> problems require the attentions of a qualified pool expert.
> These include:
>
> + A leak in the lining of the pool, whether it is
>   aboveground or in-ground.
>
> + A pump circuit that trips. You have a more serious
>   electrical problem and need to turn to a certified
>   technician.
>
> + The filter is clean, but the water is still dirty—have
>   the pump and filter housing checked out.
>
> + You cannot get leaks in tank, pump, or pipes to
>   stop, even after you've tightened the fittings.
>
> + You find sand or diatomaceous earth (depending on
>   type of filter) in pool under or near the return jets.
>
> + There are a lot of air bubbles mixing with the
>   water coming out of the return jets.
>
> + The pump makes a loud squealing noise, it heats
>   up or is not running to full capacity.
>
> + The pool is losing water even though there is no
>   apparent leak in the liner.

POWER LESS:

It's quiet poolside ... a little too quiet.

THE QUICK FIX For obvious reasons, pool power is regulated by safety measures. The problem may lie with the circuit breaker, but more often than not, the culprit will be the ground fault circuit interrupter (GFCI) outlet, where the pool equipment is plugged in. Reset the GFCI outlet (there's a red button on the outlet for just this purpose) and more than likely the power will come back on. An outdoor GFCI that trips regularly is cause for concern, however. Call an electrician if this happens.

> **DISASTER PREVENTION**
> **Pool Fences**
>
> Any pool—including aboveground models—should have a retaining fence surrounding it, with a gate that can be locked. Even if your municipality doesn't require it, you should also consider a self-closing hinge that pulls the gate shut with enough force to close the gate latch. The
>
> 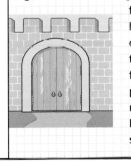 fence should be at least four feet high and sturdy enough that a child could not push it over, or slip through any openings in it (cyclone fencing is often used for this purpose). Pool fencing is a zoning requirement in many municipalities, but even where it is not, it's a wise safety measure.

8:218 | **SPARELESS MISTAKE:**

You've got a flat tire on your mountain bike, and you don't have a spare inner tube.

THE QUICK FIX Create a makeshift inner tube out of leaves and grass. "It sounds absurd, but it really works," says Scott Kaier, a mechanic at Onion River Sports in Montpelier, Vermont. "Leave one side of the tire bead hooked on the rim, and cram the opening with as much soft stuff as you can find. Install the other bead, and away you go." At least it will get you home.